SpringerBriefs in Psychology

SpringerBriefs present concise summaries of cutting-edge research and practical applications across a wide spectrum of fields. Featuring compact volumes of 50 to 125 pages, the series covers a range of content from professional to academic. Typical topics might include:

- A timely report of state-of-the-art analytical techniques
- A bridge between new research results as published in journal articles and a contextual literature review
- A snapshot of a hot or emerging topic
- An in-depth case study or clinical example
- A presentation of core concepts that readers must understand to make independent contributions

SpringerBriefs in Psychology showcase emerging theory, empirical research, and practical application in a wide variety of topics in psychology and related fields. Briefs are characterized by fast, global electronic dissemination, standard publishing contracts, standardized manuscript preparation and formatting guidelines, and expedited production schedules.

More information about this series at http://www.springer.com/series/10143

Nataliya Krasovska • Claude-Hélène Mayer

A Psychobiography of Viktor E. Frankl

Using Adversity for Life Transformation

Nataliya Krasovska
Community College
European University Viadrina
Frankfurt (Oder), Germany

Claude-Hélène Mayer
Department of Industrial Psychology and People Management
University of Johannesburg
Johannesburg, South Africa

Institut für therapeutische Kommunikation und Sprachgebrauch
Europa Universität Viadrina
Frankfurt (Oder), Germany

ISSN 2192-8363 ISSN 2192-8371 (electronic)
SpringerBriefs in Psychology
ISBN 978-3-030-70813-9 ISBN 978-3-030-70814-6 (eBook)
https://doi.org/10.1007/978-3-030-70814-6

© The Author(s), under exclusive license to Springer Nature Switzerland AG 2021

This work is subject to copyright. All rights are solely and exclusively licensed by the Publisher, whether the whole or part of the material is concerned, specifically the rights of translation, reprinting, reuse of illustrations, recitation, broadcasting, reproduction on microfilms or in any other physical way, and transmission or information storage and retrieval, electronic adaptation, computer software, or by similar or dissimilar methodology now known or hereafter developed.

The use of general descriptive names, registered names, trademarks, service marks, etc. in this publication does not imply, even in the absence of a specific statement, that such names are exempt from the relevant protective laws and regulations and therefore free for general use.

The publisher, the authors, and the editors are safe to assume that the advice and information in this book are believed to be true and accurate at the date of publication. Neither the publisher nor the authors or the editors give a warranty, expressed or implied, with respect to the material contained herein or for any errors or omissions that may have been made. The publisher remains neutral with regard to jurisdictional claims in published maps and institutional affiliations.

This Springer imprint is published by the registered company Springer Nature Switzerland AG.
The registered company address is: Gewerbestrasse 11, 6330 Cham, Switzerland

Foreword

Frankl's Cure for a Soulless Psychology and a Sick Society

Viktor Frankl, one of the most influential and enduring writers and psychotherapists of the twentieth century, continues to speak to new generations. His voice is prophetic, because it heralds the current positive psychology movement and the resurgence of spirituality and promises hope to a needy world threatened by global terrorism (Wong 2001a, b) and the AIDS epidemic (Wong 2003). However, like prophets in Biblical times, he is often misunderstood or dismissed. For example, within the positive psychology movement, especially among those who research on hope and optimism, Viktor Frankl's contributions are seldom acknowledged (Wong 2007).

Unfortunately, the above quote about Frankl remains more truthfully relevant today than two decades ago. With the mental health crisis in the era of COVID-19 (Pittaro 2020), we need Frankl's wisdom more than ever (Wong 2020a). That is why this book, *A Psychobiography of Viktor Frankl by Nataliya Krasovska and Claude-Hélène Mayer*, is both timely and important.

It is timely, because so many people are depressed, anxious, and desperate for some psychological help (Kirkey 2020) in order to overcome suffering and to restore their sanity and positive mental health. Frankl's cure seems uniquely suited for the existential crisis during the pandemic.

It is important because it explains why we need to understand Frankl's uniquely spiritual approach to healing and thriving. More specifically, it sheds light on how and why Frankl's life and wisdom on suffering provides the foundation for existential positive psychology (PP 2.0) (Wong 2011, 2019a, 2020a). In a time of death and suffering, avoidance is no longer an option. The new science of embracing what we fear may be the most promising way to save a sick society, riddled with problems of addiction, suicide, and injustice (Williamson 2020).

For many people, concepts like responsibility, self-transcendence, and suffering are much more difficult to understand and accept than happiness, success, and flourishing. It is difficult because most people view life through the lens of hedonism, materialism, and egotism. They tend to react instinctively by rejecting and avoiding anything that makes them uncomfortable. They prefer distractions or instant relief to the bitter medicine provided by Frankl. However, when none of the quick fixes has worked and the society as a whole is broken, why not give Frankl a chance? His wisdom on suffering is worth listening to because he has overcome hardships and traumas much worse than we can imagine.

Frankl's Struggles and the Development of Logotherapy

As a Jew living in Vienna, Frankl sought to assimilate into the majority of his society, aspiring to be among the metropolitan elite, but still had to struggle with the issue of maintaining his own cultural identity. This resulted in developing an open-minded approach to integrate opposing ideas. Such an integrative approach paved the way for the broad appeal of logotherapy.

He went through the great depression of the 1930s and two world wars, being under Nazi occupation as well as in Nazi concentration camps. He also had to work through the grief of losing his wife and family, the collective guilt of collaboration with the Hitler's regime, and the reality of facing death up close and personal as a Jew and a physician. In addition, as a precocious child, his first encounter with the terror of death was when he was 4-year old: Throughout his teenage years, he struggled with the meaning of life in the face of death (Pytell 2020). This led to his conclusion that it is difficult to live a meaningful life without some understanding of the meaning of death and suffering.

As a very intelligent and creative person, he aspired to learn from the best. He studied with Freud and Adler, the two greatest psychotherapists at his time about the genesis of mental illness and its cure. He had to struggle between getting full acceptance into their school of thought and speaking up about the shortcomings of their approaches. In the end, he chose to remain true to his own conviction and values.

Between Freud's individualism and Adler's communalism, Frankl chose the third way—to develop a "height psychology" in which an individual is held accountable to a higher authority for living a socially productive life. Thus, the individual is absorbed in the community, and yet still personally responsible for charting one's own authentic path. To him, this is the best way to avoid the extremes of nihilism and abuse of personal freedom and the authoritarianism of Hitler's fascism or Stalin's Marxism. He discovered the universal balancing principle to arrive at the middle way.

Therefore, his logotherapy (therapy through meaning), a fundamental part of the Third Viennese School of Psychotherapy, has something very unique to offer to the world. He repeatedly emphasized that logotherapy is a spiritual therapy because his own spiritual struggles at the Nazi death camps revealed to him that the horrors of the Holocaust were also an opportunity to discover the ultimate meaning through faith in

God (Frankl 2000). This faith provides the grounding for objective values and meaning in the face of death as well as the necessary spiritual fiber to say "yes" to life no matter what. Thus, while cognitive psychology restored the mind to psychology, Frankl's logotherapy restored the spirit or the soul to psychology as the noetic dimension of personhood.

Frankl reasoned that since life was surrounded by death in the Nazi concentration camps, the meaning of life could not be derived from the pleasure principle or the power principle. Therefore, it could only be derived from outside the person—something transcendental. The will to meaning is a spiritual act of volition to direct one's life toward transcendental goals in order to rise above the evitable suffering and death (Frankl 1988).

Through his prolific writings, especially through his own life, Frankl has demonstrated compellingly that meaning in terms of the pursuit of self-transcendence is the most promising way to survive and thrive in a difficult and dangerous world. Even for those who do not believe in a personal God, they can still understand self-transcendence as a spiritual resource essential in overcoming suffering and death (Maslow 1971; Smith and Liehr 2018).

To both Frankl and Maslow, self-transcendence represents the highest values. Maslow (1971) has provided a comprehensive definition:

> Transcendence refers to the very highest and most inclusive or holistic levels of human consciousness, behaving and relating, as ends rather than means, to oneself, to significant others, to human beings in general, to other species, to nature, and to the cosmos (p. 269).

The Vital Role of Meaning in Well-being and Success

According to Frankl (1946/1985a):

> The meaning of life is to be discovered in the world rather than within man or his own psyche, as though it were a closed system. It denotes the fact that being human always points, and is directed, to something, or someone, other than oneself—be it a meaning to fulfill or another human being to encounter. The more one forgets himself—by giving himself to a cause to serve or another person to love—the more human he is and the more he actualizes himself. What is called self-actualization is not an attainable aim at all, for the simple reason that the more one would strive for it, the more he would miss it. In other words, self-actualization is possible only as a side-effect of self-transcendence. (pp. 110–111)

This book shows us how Frankl's personal history and the social cultural milieu of his time interacted to shape his noble view of human life and the key concepts of logotherapy—the tragic triad (pain, guilt, and death) and the spiritual triad (freedom of the will, will to meaning, and meaning of life).

These spiritual laws are needed to transform the tragic triad into the light triad of *responsibility* to repent and make positive changes, *conscience* to do what is right by transcending one's egotistic and deterministic forces, and *faith* in the ultimate meaning of life and God. The alternative reaction to the tragic triad, according to egotistic desires or the voice of the Devil, is maladaptive and may result in the dark triad of narcissism, psychopathy, and Machiavellianism.

From his own experience, Frankl discovered the spiritual transformation of the tragic triad. Guilt and shame over wrongdoing can be best wiped out by taking personal responsibility: to repent and own up to one's mistakes, and to make positive changes to redeem oneself. Thus, personal responsibility is the key to repairing the worst and bringing out the best in any individual. One cannot have rebirth without death to the old self. Each person "has to answer to life answering for life; he has to respond by being responsible; in other words, the response is necessarily a response-in-action" (Frankl 2000, p. 29). Thus, one can live a second time as if one has lived wrongly the first time.

Alternatively, if one covers up their guilt and shame by overcompensating and resorting to one's will to power and superiority complex, one becomes a narcissist, who is always anxious of being exposed as an imposter. For example, when one feels guilt for not getting a task done, then any gentle reminder of this delinquency will be interpreted as a scolding or a personal attack and will be met by an angry reaction resulting in an unnecessary fight. Thus, avoiding one's responsibility can lead to personal anxiety and toxic behavior toward others.

With respect to suffering and pain, one needs to follow one's conscience, which helps discover the best way to respond to them in a socially worthwhile way. As we exercise the will to meaning, invariably, the "unconscious God" (Frankl 1946/1985b) would reveal the highest value of self-transcendence, the objective value to serving someone bigger than oneself.

Alternatively, one resorts to scapegoating and demonizing others for one's suffering. This leads to aggression and psychopathy. One may also resort to becoming addicted to drugs, alcohol, or food as a way to escape from suffering. Either way, egotistic ways of coping with suffering contribute to psychopathology. A more sinister scheme is to destroy others who are more successful; it would lead to the evil of hurting others without benefiting one's self as demonstrated in mass killings or terrorism.

Finally, with respect to death or the finitude of life, the only effective antidote is to make the best use of one's available time on earth and to believe that life has intrinsic and ultimate meaning, no matter what. This affirmation of life stems from one's faith in God and in one's own unique worth.

The alternative of trying to get as much as one can, regardless of legal and ethical consequences, inevitably leads to Machiavellianism, which often accompanies narcissism and psychopathy. This may lead to pathological lying, betrayal, double-crossing, sabotaging, and corrupting due processes. That is why we have so many leaders in corporations and politics clearly showing characteristics of the dark triad (Furtner et al. 2017; Morin 2019).

At present, we really have a leadership crisis in our government and corporations. Frankl's emphasis on conscience, objective values, and highest ideals is much needed in leadership and management. He shows us the wisdom of living and behaving as if there is a God to whom we are all accountable. Frankl's light triad provides a cure for a society drunk in its mad pursuit of pleasure, power, and pride at the expense of innocent and vulnerable people. It is an empirical question whether Frankl's spiritually oriented light triad has different correlates from Kaufman et al.'s (2019) humanistically oriented light triad; regardless, there is the need to focus on the light forces and overcome the dark forces to make this world a better place.

In addition, Frankl has successfully resolved several existential issues facing individuals, especially leaders. For example, for the ontological dilemma of staying the same vs. making changes for a better future, Frankl argues for taking the risk of moving forward with the risks of uncertainty and possible failure because life is not about maintaining the status quo or hemostasis, but about growing and embracing the necessary tension and risks of life expansion—this is what makes us feel fully alive. His logic is that human beings are an open system in a complex evolving society, where the only constant is change. That is why we need to have the courage to embrace change in order to move forward. It is like the Chinese saying: when we paddle upstream, not moving forward is going backward. Progress always involves a struggle and overcoming risks and setbacks.

Another common existential issue is realism vs. idealism or meaning vs. expedience. We want to pursue our dreams, but we also need to survive and make a living. Frankl's answer to this dilemma is that it all depends on the context or situation. For example, he chose to compromise in order to practice medicine in Nazi-controlled hospitals or psychological institutes. He has been criticized for working for the Nazis (Pytell 2020). But the alternative might have been the end of his brilliant career or personal death. Most scientists had to somewhat compromise their values in order to work in Nazi Germany or Nazi-controlled Europe, because open resistance is not only futile but suicidal.

It is unfortunate that Frankl's ideas have not been taken seriously by researchers in mainstream psychology, probably due to his emphasis on the spiritual dimension. I hope that this book will help change this bias by showing us how Frankl discovered the paradoxical truth from his own suffering, and that a tragic sense of life is the necessary foundation for healing and flourishing in spite of suffering, guilt, and death (Frankl 1946/1985a; Unamuno 2014).

Wong's Extension of Frankl's Work into PP 2.0

Born in war-torn China and facing discrimination and marginalization as a racial minority in North America (Wong 2020b), it is natural that I really resonate with Frankl's writing. I had the privilege of talking to him several times while working on The Human Crisis for meaning (Wong and Fry 1998). I also worked closely with Joseph Fabry (Wong 1999).

I have taken on the mission to translate Frankl's concepts to testable models (Wong 2007, 2012). More specifically, I have expanded Frankl's work in two directions: (a) PP 2.0 as a theoretical framework for research and practice (Wong 2011, 2016a) and (b) integrative meaning therapy (Wong 2009, 2016b).

Based on Frankl's teaching and my own lifelong research (2019b), the following summarizes the main three insights from PP 2.0:

(1) *True positivity is the ability to see the light in the darkness.* Cultivating the resilient mindset (Wong 2020) and the attitude of tragic optimism (Leung 2019; Wong 2001) allows one to see the bright side of the worst situation and suffering as a blessing in disguise (Jans-Beken and Wong 2019). This ability needs to be awakened and stretched. Such effort is worth it because it results in sustainable positive mental health even during the worst circumstances.
(2) *True success is to embrace the dark side and turn it into the foundation for achieving one's highest value.* The next step is to strive toward one's dream made up of one's highest ideals. This will involve coping with the difficulties and failures by developing the necessary resources according to the deep and wide hypothesis (Wong and Worth 2017) following the resource-congruence model of effective coping (Wong et al. 2006). With problems that are beyond human control, the most congruent way of coping is religious coping and meaning-focused coping.
(3) *The good life is a balancing act of navigating between opposite forces in each situation.* This would require practicing the dual-system model (Wong 2012) or the Yin–Yang dialectic to maintain a dynamic balance between two opposite forces. Sustainable mature happiness can be achieved through the practical wisdom and the successful managing of the opponent process of Yin–Yang (Wong and Bowers 2018).

The above three principles can also be expressed as the four basic tenets of PP 2.0:

1. Embrace the dark side of life as the other half of complete circle of well-being.
2. Practice the Yin–Yang dialectic as the way to achieve optimal balance and harmony in life.
3. Facing life with the meaning mindset and the resilient mindset is a precondition for resilience and flourishing.
4. Pursuing meaning (self-transcendence) is the most promising way to achieve self-actualization and fulfillment.

Paradoxically, when we are courageous and humble enough to remove all our personas and defense mechanisms, and embrace suffering openly, we will be liberated from the negative emotions surrounding the initial wounding, such as fear, anger, and resentment, and be free to pursue faith, meaning, and love needed for personal growth. In this inward journey, we not only find healing but also our destiny to become what we were meant to be—a self-transcending human being (Wong 2016).

The added value of the psychobiography of Frankl is that it shows how the best tenets of Wong's PP 2.0 are related to Frankl's key concepts of responsibility, will to meaning, and self-transcendence. In terms of practice, PP 2.0 also emphasizes the will to power or the mental muscle of self-control.

I want to propose 12 exercises to build up your spiritual fiber and mental muscles so that you can face whatever life throws at you without losing your balance and serenity and develop the light triad according to Frankl's three avenues of value—creative value, experiential value, and attitudinal value (Frankl 1946/1985a):

1. Know the difference between right and wrong and always do what is right according to your beliefs, core values, and practical wisdom.
2. Have the courage or defiant attitude to stand up to the dark forces even when they are beyond your control.
3. Know your vulnerabilities and what upsets you most. Try to practice facing what you fear or hate most until you learn how to accept it with equanimity because it really does not matter when death comes.
4. Be prepared for the worst so that you can take measures to prevent it from happening and you will not be shocked when it does happen.
5. Believe that you can turn every setback to your advantage and accomplish your goal eventually, even though the situation looks hopeless.
6. Keep your ritual for stillness (or wu wei) whether it is meditation, prayer, tai chi, or spending time with nature. Do it as often as you can. It is the time to experience solitude and quietness, to clear your mind of the endless chatter, and to recharge your battery.
7. Train your mind to focus on the task at hand so that you will not ruminate over troublesome issues or worry about negative outcomes.
8. Discipline yourself so that you know how to balance work with play, caring for others and the self, and realism and idealism.
9. Refuse to waste your time with toxic people and refuse to allow them to rob you of your inner peace.
10. Stop chasing after happiness; instead, learn to maintain a positive mental state of calm and deep joy in spite of the constant presence of stress and pressure.
11. Appreciate all your experiences, both positive or negative.
12. Keep the fire burning in your belly so that you can persevere in pursuing your dreams.

Peterborough, Canada   Paul T. P. Wong

References

Frankl, V.E. 1946/1985a. *Man's search for meaning*. Washington Square Press.
———. 1946/1985b. *The unconscious God*. Pocket Books.
———. 1988. *The will to meaning: foundations and applications of logotherapy*. New York: Meridian Books.
———. 2000. *Man's search for ultimate meaning*. New York: Barnes and Noble.
Furtner, M.R., T. Maran, and J.F. Rauthmann. 2017. Dark leadership: The role of leaders' dark triad personality traits. In *Leader development deconstructed. Annals of theoretical psychology*, ed. M. Clark, and C. Gruber, vol 15. Cham: Springer. https://doi.org/10.1007/978-3-319-64740-1_4

Jans-Beken, L.G.P.J., and P.T.P. Wong. 2019. Development and preliminary validation of the Existential Gratitude Scale (EGS). *Counselling Psychology Quarterly*. Advance online publication. https://doi.org/10.1080/09515070.2019.1656054

Kaufman, S.B., D.B. Yaden, E. Hyde, and E. Tsukayama. 2019. The light vs. dark triad of personality: Contrasting two very different profiles of human nature. *Frontiers in Psychology* 10: 467. https://doi.org/10.3389/fpsyg.2019.00467

Kirkey, S. 2020. More than 200 days in, COVID-19 is taking a psychological toll and that's entirely normal. *National Post*. https://nationalpost.com/health/more-than-200-days-in-covid-19-is-taking-a-psychological-toll-and-thats-entirely-normal

Leung, M.M. 2019. Tragic optimism: An integrative meaning-centred approach to trauma treatment. *Counselling Psychology Quarterly*. Advance online publication. https://doi.org/10.1080/09515070.2019.1633497

Maslow, A.H. 1971. *The farther reaches of human nature*. Arkana/Penguin Books.

Morin, T. 2019. Dark leadership is killing organizations and making us miserable. *Work Feels Good*. https://workfeelsgood.com/dark-leadership/

Pittaro, M. 2020. Crisis fatigue and the COVID-19 pandemic. *Psychology Today*. https://www.psychologytoday.com/ca/blog/the-crime-and-justice-doctor/202008/crisis-fatigue-and-the-covid-19-pandemic

Pytell, T. 2020. *Victor Frankl's search for meaning: an emblematic 20th-century life*. Berghahn Books.

Smith, M.J., and P.R. Liehr, eds. 2018. *Middle range theory for nursing* (4th ed.). Springer Publishing Company. (See Reed's chapter on self-transcendence)

Unamuno, M. 2014. *Tragic sense of life*. CreateSpace Independent Publishing Platform.

Williamson, M. 2020. The origins of America's mental health crisis. *Newsweek*. https://www.newsweek.com/marianne-williamson-origins-americas-mental-health-crisis-opinion-1539782

Wong, P.T. 2001. Tragic optimism, realistic pessimism, and mature happiness: An existential model. *Positive Psychology Summit, Washington, DC*.

Wong, P.T.P. 1999. Joseph Fabry: A visionary storyteller. *International Network on Personal Meaning*. Retrieved from http://www.meaning.ca/therapy/therapists/Ther_pages/joseph_fabry.htm

———. 2007. Viktor Frankl: Prophet of hope for the 21st century. *Meaning.ca* https://www.meaning.ca/article/viktor-frankl-prophet-hope-herald-positive-psychology/

———. 2009. Meaning therapy: an integrative and positive existential psychotherapy. *Journal of Contemporary Psychotherapy*, 40, 85–93. https://link.springer.com/article/10.1007/s10879-009-9132-6

———. 2011. Positive psychology 2.0: Towards a balanced interactive model of the good life. *Canadian Psychology/Psychologie canadienne* 52(2): 69–81. https://doi.org/10.1037/a0022511

———. 2012. Toward a dual-systems model of what makes life worth living. In *The human quest for meaning: Theories, research, and applications*, ed. P. T. P. Wong (2nd ed., 3–22). New York, NY: Routledge.

———. 2012. What is the meaning mindset? *International Journal of Existential Psychology and Psychotherapy* 4(1): 1–3.

———. 2014. Viktor Frankl's meaning seeking model and positive psychology. In *Meaning in existential and positive psychology*, ed. A. Batthyany and P. Russo-Netzer, 149–184). New York: Springer.

———. 2016. Self-transcendence: A paradoxical way to become your best. *International Journal of Existential Psychology and Psychotherapy* 6(1). Retrieved from http://journal.existentialpsychology.org/index.php/ExPsy/article/view/178/141

———. 2016a. Existential positive psychology. *International Journal of Existential Psychology and Psychotherapy*, 6(1). Retrieved from http://journal.existentialpsychology.org/index.php/ExPsy/article/view/179/158

———. 2016b. Integrative meaning therapy: From logotherapy to existential positive interventions. In *Clinical perspectives on meaning: Positive and existential psychotherapy*, ed. P. Russo-Netzer, S.E. Schulenberg, and A. Batthyány, 323–342. New York, NY: Springer.

———. 2019a. Second wave positive psychology's (PP 2.0) contribution to counselling psychology. *Counselling Psychology Quarterly* [Special Issue]. Retrieved from https://doi.org/10.1080/09515070.2019.1671320

———. 2019b. Why and how I developed the positive psychology of suffering. *Dr. Paul T. P. Wong*. Retrieved from http://www.drpaulwong.com/why-and-how-i-developed-the-positive-psychology-of-suffering/

———. 2020a. *Made for resilience and happiness: Effective coping with COVID-19 according to Viktor E. Frankl and Paul T. P. Wong*. Toronto, ON: INPM Press.

———. 2020b. The unheard cry of a successful Asian psychologist. *The Journal of Psychology: Interdisciplinary and Applied*. https://doi.org/10.1080/00223980.2020.1820430

Wong, P.T.P., and V. Bowers. 2018. Mature happiness and global wellbeing in difficult times. In *Scientific concepts behind happiness, kindness, and empathy in contemporary society*, ed. N.R. Silton. Hershey, PA: IGI Global.

Wong, P.T.P., and P.S. Fry, ed. 1998. *The human quest for meaning: A handbook of psychological research and clinical applications*. Mahwah, NJ: Erlbaum.

Wong, P.T.P., and P. Worth. 2017. The deep-and-wide hypothesis in giftedness and creativity [Special issue]. *Psychology and Education* 54(3/4). Retrieved from http://www.psychologyandeducation.net/pae/category/volume-54-no-3-4-2017/

Wong, P.T.P., G.T. Reker, and E. Peacock. 2006. The resource-congruence model of coping and the development of the Coping Schemas Inventory. In *Handbook of multicultural perspectives on stress and coping*, ed. P.T.P. Wong, and L.C.J. Wong, 223–283). New York, NY: Springer.

Endorsements

"This is a rigorously conducted psychobiography of one of the greatest existential minds of the 20th century. Using the theoretical lens of Positive Psychology 2.0, and incorporating best methodological practices, Krasovska and Mayer have provided a clear window into the inner psychology of Viktor Frankl as he honed his therapeutic model in the midst of his concentration camps experiences. An enlightening, riveting psychological profile of one of history's greatest existential thinkers and practitioners, Viktor Frankl."

—Joseph G. Ponterotto, Ph.D., Psychologist and Psychobiographer, Professor of Counseling Psychology, *Fordham University, New York City*

"This captivating historical and psychological booklet on the life of holocaust survivor, Victor Frankl, finely illustrates the use of adversity for life transformation. Surviving the Shoah (the genocide of victims of Nazi persecution) demanded character strengths grounded within transcendent virtues of beauty, gratitude, hope, humor, and spirituality. This psycho-historical book by renowned psychobiographers, Krasovska and Mayer, reconstructs the life of Frankl during his childhood and adolescent years, before, during, and after his confinement in concentration camps. It particularly illustrates life transformation according to the second wave of Positive Psychology, advocated by Professor Paul Wong. It is a must-read for anyone interested in life adversity and ways to transform your life into a person with transcendent virtues."

—Paul J. Fouché, Full Professor in Psychology, *University of the Free State, Bloemfontain, South Africa*

About this Book

This psychobiography on the life of Viktor Frankl is an exploratory-descriptive study that aims to explore and describe Viktor Frankl's life according to the theory of Positive Psychology 2.0 (PP2.0) of Paul Wong. The method of research uses a qualitative single-case research design that studies Frankl's life during his childhood and adolescent years, especially before, during, and after his stay in concentration camps.

A purposive sampling procedure was used to select Viktor Frankl as the subject of the research, and only published data was analyzed. The researcher used the content analysis in order to reduce text and find out relevant information while applying subjective sense-making. Multiple sources of data are used to obtain the information in this research, including selected autobiographic books and biographies written by different authors. This data is organized according to the temporal sequence of Viktor Frankl's life span and the two tenets of PP 2.0 such as virtue and meaning. Since the term virtue is extensive, this research deals only with the character strengths of transcendent virtues such as appreciation of beauty, gratitude, hope, humor, and spirituality. Paul Wong's PURE model is used to analyze the structure of meaning in Viktor Frankl's life. In order to highlight unusual and important life events, Alexander's primary indicators of psychological salience and Schultz's "prototypical scenes" were also applied in this study.

Contents

1	**Introduction**	1
	1.1 Chapter Preview	1
	1.2 An Overview of the Psychobiographical Approach	1
	1.3 A Brief Introduction to Viktor Frankl's Life	2
	1.4 Overview of the Theoretical Framework for This Study	4
	1.5 Research Methodology	4
	1.6 Purpose, Aims, and Contribution of the Research	5
	1.7 The Motivation for the Research Study	5
	1.8 Outline of the Structure of This Study	6
	1.9 Chapter Conclusion	7
	References	7
2	**Psychobiography: A Theoretical Overview**	9
	2.1 Chapter Preview	9
	2.2 Psychobiography: Definition and Its Aims	9
	2.3 The History of Psychobiography	10
	2.4 The Value and Contribution of Psychobiographical Case Studies	11
	2.5 Conclusion	12
	References	12
3	**Viktor Frankl: Life and Works**	13
	3.1 Chapter Preview	13
	3.2 Early Years	13
	3.3 Theresienstadt	19
	3.4 Auschwitz	21
	3.4.1 The Phase of Shock	21
	3.4.2 Apathy and Lessons of Survival	22
	3.5 Postwar Years	24
	3.6 Chapter Summary	26
	References	27

4 Positive Psychology 2.0 of Paul Wong ... 29
- 4.1 Chapter Preview ... 29
- 4.2 The Principles of Positive Psychology 2.0 ... 29
- 4.3 Central Tenets of Positive Psychology 2.0 ... 30
  - 4.3.1 Virtues ... 30
  - 4.3.2 The Virtue of Transcendence ... 31
  - 4.3.3 Meaning ... 32
- 4.4 The Need for Positive Psychology in the Context of Psychobiography ... 33
- 4.5 Conclusion ... 33
- References ... 34

5 Research Design and Methodology ... 37
- 5.1 Chapter Preview ... 37
- 5.2 The Research Design and Process in Psychobiography ... 37
- 5.3 Data Collection ... 38
- 5.4 Data Analysis and Interpretation ... 38
  - 5.4.1 Content Analysis ... 39
  - 5.4.2 Alexander's Indicators of Psychological Saliency ... 39
  - 5.4.3 Schultz's Prototypical Scenes ... 40
- 5.5 Good Psychobiography Markers ... 41
- 5.6 Chapter Summary ... 42
- References ... 42

6 Research Findings on Viktor Frankl's Life ... 43
- 6.1 Chapter Preview ... 43
- 6.2 The Virtue of Transcendence ... 43
  - 6.2.1 Childhood and Youth ... 44
  - 6.2.2 Before the Concentration Camps ... 45
  - 6.2.3 During the Concentration Camps ... 47
  - 6.2.4 After the Concentration Camps ... 49
- 6.3 Meaning ... 51
  - 6.3.1 Before the Concentration Camps ... 51
  - 6.3.2 During the Concentration Camps ... 53
  - 6.3.3 After the Concentration Camps ... 54
- 6.4 Alexander's Indicators of Psychological Salience ... 57
- 6.5 Schultz's Prototypical Scenes ... 61
- 6.6 Chapter Conclusion ... 63
- References ... 63

7 Discussion of Results ... 65
- 7.1 Chapter Preview ... 65
- 7.2 The Virtue of Transcendence ... 65
  - 7.2.1 Appreciation of Beauty ... 65
  - 7.2.2 Gratitude ... 66

		7.2.3	Hope	66
		7.2.4	Humour	67
		7.2.5	Spirituality	67
	7.3	Meaning		68
		7.3.1	Purpose	68
		7.3.2	Understanding	69
		7.3.3	Responsible Action	69
		7.3.4	Enjoyment and Evaluation	70
	7.4	Alexander's Indicators of Psychological Salience		70
	7.5	Schultz's Prototypical Scenes		72
	7.6	Conclusion		72
	References			73
8	**Conclusions**			75
	8.1	Chapter Preview		75
	8.2	Summary of the Research Findings		75
	8.3	The Limitations of this Research		76
	8.4	The Value of this Research		76
	8.5	Recommendations for Further Research		77
	8.6	Conclusion		77
	References			77

Chapter 1
Introduction

1.1 Chapter Preview

This chapter provides an introduction to the psychobiographical study on Viktor Frankl. The study uses Wong's (2011, 2019, 2020a, b) theory of Positive Psychology 2.0 (PP2.0) to illustrate the life of Viktor Frankl, an Austrian neurologist and psychiatrist as well as a Holocaust survivor who developed his own theory of the will to meaning as a mean to overcome suffering and adversity. This chapter introduces the psychobiographical approach to research in the field of psychology and provides a brief account of Frankl's life. An overview of Wong's (Wong 2011, 2019, 2020a, b) theory is also provided to orientate the reader to the theoretical structure that guided the process of data collection and the study itself. It emphasizes finally the researcher's motivation regarding the research study (the emic perspective) and provides an overview of the structure of the study (the etic outside).

1.2 An Overview of the Psychobiographical Approach

Psychobiography is a qualitative research methodology which aims at understanding individual lives, uniqueness and exceptionality of people, and how they function (Schultz 2005b). There are two reasons for doing a psychobiography: "to cogently know another person, and to know ourselves" (Schultz 2005b). In order to conduct psychobiographical research, the relevant psychological theory should be used. Therefore, psychobiography is "the systematic use of psychological (especially personality) theory to transform a life into a coherent and illuminating story" (McAdams 1988). The psychobiographical analysis produces insights and inspiration for new formal propositions that can be tested against larger groups of people (Schultz 2005b). It means that psychobiographies may serve as a resource for the new psychological theories and hypotheses (Mayer and Kováry 2019; Mayer and

Fouché 2021). Moreover, psychobiography as a case study can help to prove or facilitate an existing psychological theory (Schultz 2005a, b, c, d; Yin 2014).

This study focuses on and explores the life of Viktor Frankl based on Paul Wong's theory of PP 2.0 (Chap. 4) as well as Alexander's indicators of psychological salience (Sect. 5.4.2) and Schultz's prototypical scenes (Sect. 5.4.3). In this chapter, an overview of the life, theories and research methodology is outlined to provide the reader with the orientation to this psychobiographical study.

1.3 A Brief Introduction to Viktor Frankl's Life

Reviews of Viktor Frankl's life can be found in texts by Längle (2013), Soggie (2016), Frankl (1984, 2000, 2015), Klingberg (2013). He was born 26.03.1905 in Vienna, Austria in a Jewish family of civil servants. As a child, Viktor Frankl asked himself the question about human mortality and the meaning of life (Längle 2013). Before falling asleep, he often thought about death and the transitory nature of life, which seemed to him to destroy its meaning (Frankl 2000).

Frankl described himself as a seeker of knowledge, interested in philosophers and in experiments (Frankl 2000). Until junior high, Frankl was on the school honour rolls, but then he began to follow his own interests (Frankl 2000). As a 14-year-schoolboy, he began taking adult evening classes in applied psychology and brought the lessons back to his school classroom for demonstrations (Frankl 2000). In these lectures, he developed the idea that humans should not ask what a meaning of life is, rather life is asking us this question, "What is the meaning of this life?". It is we who must answer this question on an everyday basis (Frankl 2000).

Frankl gave his first lecture on the meaning of life when he was just 15 years old (Längle 2013). Later, in 1923, the 18-year-old Frankl published his first article in the Youth supplement of a daily newspaper (Längle 2013).

At the age of 19, Frankl made two steps toward his dream of becoming a doctor: he was admitted into medical school and joined Sigmund Freud's Vienna Psychoanalytic Society (Soggie 2016). However, Frankl became disappointed with psychoanalysis as it did not satisfy his longing to understand people. He found himself increasingly interested by the Individualistic Psychology of Alfred Adler (Soggie 2016).

After graduating from medical school in the year of 1930, Viktor went on to specialize in general psychiatry and neurology (Frankl 2000).

In the late 1930s, the Nazi influence was growing within Austria. In September 1939, Viktor Frankl was the only sibling of the Frankl family who remained with his parents in Vienna, supporting them with whatever he could (Frankl 2000).

In 1942, Frankl and his family were transported to Theresienstadt (Soggie 2016). Viktor, his parents and wife, could not live together in the camp because there were separate living quarters for young, the elderly, women, and men (Soggie 2016). In Theresienstadt, Frankl was assigned to special duties as a doctor. He was to oversee a group of sick people. This task allowed him to see his family every day (Soggie

2016). In 1943, Viktor Frankl's father died of starvation and pneumonia being 81 years old (Längle 2013). In 1944, Frankl appeared on the list of those being moved to other camps. Tilly Frankl volunteered to go with him, although Viktor Frankl was against this decision, as this place could be worst then Theresienstadt (Klingberg 2013). Frankl's 65-year-old mother remained in Theresienstadt (Klingberg 2013) Viktor Frankl hoped she would survive by avoiding transport and staying at Theresienstadt (Klingberg 2013). However, she was also transported to Auschwitz and murdered in the gas chamber on the 23.10.1944 (Längle 2013).

In 1944, Viktor Frankl was deported with his wife to Poland, Auschwitz in a camp called Birkenau (Soggie 2016). The conditions were worse than those at Theresienstadt, the camp was overcrowded, and water and sanitation were not enough what resulted in the rapid spread of disease (Soggie 2016). Harsh circumstances did not discourage Frankl from developing his theory of meaning further (Soggie 2016).

In August 1945, 4 months after his liberation, Frankl returned to Vienna (Soggie 2016). The city was ruined; the Jewish community was gone (Soggie 2016). He then found out about the death of his wife Tilly, his mother, brother, and his sister-in-law (Soggie 2016). Viktor suffered from moral deformity, bitterness and disillusionment as he tried to return to his former life (Soggie 2016).

Frankl tried to resolve his soul collapse by the writing of a book. Längle (2013) reports that works that he created during these years constitute the basis of his scientific life's work. "The doctor and the Soul" and "Man's Search For Meaning" (originally published as Nevertheless, Say "Yes" to Life: A Psychologist Experiences the Concentration Camp) were released in 1946 (Längle 2013).

In 1946 Frankl became acquainted with his second wife: Eleonore Katharina. In 1949, Frankl became a father for the first and only time (Längle 2013). In the year of her birth, Frankl dedicated the book "The unconditional human being—Metaclinical Lectures" to his daughter (Längle 2013).

Since Frankl's lectures were very successful and his concentration camp book sold well in the U.S, he embarked on tremendous lecturing activity, which made him a top-rated speaker in the 1960 years, first in English-speaking countries and eventually worldwide (Längle 2013). He undertook a hundred lecture tours in America alone; four of them went around the world. There were eventually more than 200 universities outside Europe where Frankl held lectures (Längle 2013). More and more frequently, prominent figures from politics and science invited him, such as Pope Paul VI (Längle 2013).

In the last months of his life, his heart became significantly worse (Längle 2013). The physicians confronted him with the decision to either undertake a risky operation or very likely die of heart failure (Längle 2013). Frankl opted for surgery during which he died, on 2.09.1997 (Längle 2013).

1.4 Overview of the Theoretical Framework for This Study

Paul Wong's (2011) model of Positive Psychology, called Positive Psychology 2.0 (further named PP 2.0), will guide this study. According to Wong (2011), classical Positive Psychology does not provide a comprehensive answer to the question what to do with negative emotions and experiences emphasizing just positive effects, experiences and emotions. Therefore, Wong suggests a balanced model of Positive Psychology, called Positive Psychology 2.0, where both sides, positive and negative experiences as well as strengths and weaknesses of people, are integrated (Wong 2011). Such an approach enables us to understand the complexity of life in its totality (Wong 2011, 2019.).

Wong provides the Four Pillars of PP 2.0 such as virtue, meaning, resilience and well-being (Wong 2011). For the sake of space, this study focuses on the first two pillars in Frankl's life as it unfolded during his childhood, before, during and after staying in concentration camps.

According to McCullough and Snyder (2000), virtue is a "psychological process that consistently enables a person to think and act so as to yield benefits to him or herself and society" [1]. The virtue of transcendence is defined as "strengths that forge connections to the larger universe and provide meaning" (Peterson and Seligman 2004). Peterson and Seligman (2004) provide the following character strengths which define the virtue of transcendence: an appreciation of beauty and excellence, gratitude, hope, humour and spirituality.

In order to explain the structure and functions of meaning, P. T. P. Wong (2010) suggests the PURE-Model which stands for Purpose, Understanding, Responsible Action and Enjoyment. These components will be used in the study to systematically describe how the meaning in Viktor Frankl's life was created, lived through and evaluated by himself.

1.5 Research Methodology

According to Runyan (1988a, b), a psychobiography can be described as research of a life history. This type of study uses a qualitative single-case research design (Yin 2003) which explores the life of Viktor Frankl during his childhood, adolescent years as well as the period before, during and after concentration camps. The data collection process in this psychobiographical case study is based on the distinction of Allport (1961), who differentiates between first-person and third-person documents. The following first-person documents are used: "Recollections: An Autobiography" (2000), "Man's Search For Meaning" (1984), private letters of V. Frankl from the book "Es kommt der Tag, da bist du frei" ("There will come a day when you are free") (2015). The following third-person documents are used in this study: Längle, A. (2013) "Viktor Frankl: Eine Begegnung" (Viktor Frankl: An Encounter), Soggie, N. A. (2016) "Logotherapy. Viktor Frankl, Life and Work".

1.7 The Motivation for the Research Study 5

In this study, content analysis (Yin 2014) is used to identify "key issues" based on the model of PP 2.0 of Wong (2011) in the data throughout the life span of Viktor Frankl. According to Krippendorff (2013), "content analysis is a research technique for making replicable and valid inferences from texts (or other meaningful matter) to the contexts of their use" [24]. Mayer (2017) states that a content analysis displays a subjective process between the researcher and the texts. In this study, content analysis is used to make replicable and valid inferences about the life of Viktor Frankl applying the pre-defined categories such as "virtue" and "meaning" deriving from the main tenets of PP 2.0 of Paul T. P. Wong. This study also uses Alexander's primary indicators of psychological salience (see Schultz 2005c) and Schultz's prototypical scenes (Schultz 2005c) in order to receive an in-depth view into the personality of Viktor Frankl.

The data analysis in this study is conducted through the five-step process of content analysis by Blanche et al. (2006). It involves familiarization and immersion into the texts, inducing themes, coding, elaboration, interpretation and checking of the results.

1.6 Purpose, Aims, and Contribution of the Research

The primary aim of this study is to explore the life of Viktor Frankl according to Wong's (2011) model of PP 2.0 and answer the question how character strengths of transcendent virtue contributed to Frank's ability to stay resilient towards suffering and find meaning in negative life situations. The study's purpose is to provide a new understanding and perspective on the person of Viktor Frankl in the context of Alexander's primary indicators of psychological salience (see Schultz 2005c) and Schultz's prototypical scenes (Schultz 2005c).

1.7 The Motivation for the Research Study

The researchers' motivation to write the psychobiographical study on the life of Viktor Frankl is based on their interest in the effective strategies in dealing with challenging life situations and developing resiliency through suffering, pain and despair (van Tongeren and Showalter van Tongeren 2020).

The life of Viktor Frankl was replete with suffering and pain (Wong 2020a, b). However, he was able to overcome suffering, develop insight into his life mission and find meaning in adversity. The key interest of the researchers' were the following questions: which factors influenced the ability of V. Frankl to see positive meaning in suffering and pain? Which life principles and narratives accompanied Frankl throughout his life? How can virtue of transcendence contribute to a person's ability to overcome life's hardships? Which role does the virtue of transcendence play in finding life meaning and leading a fulfilling life? Moreover, the researcher aimed at an in-depth analysis of the personality of Viktor Frankl, his character traits and beliefs. The researcher asked herself about the possible side effects of Frankl's positive traits in order to create a full picture of his personality.

1.8 Outline of the Structure of This Study

This research is divided into eight chapters. In the second chapter, the theoretical review on psychobiography is given. Based on the works of W. T. Schultz, J. G. Ponterotto, W. M. Ruyan, Z. Kováry, Mayer and Kováry, the psychobiography, its main terms and definitions are introduced. The history of psychobiographical research, as well as its value and contribution, are presented.

Chapter 3 provides the biographical information on V. Frankl. As the researcher's interest lies in the coping strategies and the process of finding meaning in adversities, the most challenging life phases of V. Frankl such as life in a concentration camp and after his liberation are introduced more detailed. However, the family background, historical context as well as adolescent years of Viktor Frankl are considered in order to provide the holistic picture of the analyzed person.

In Chap. 4, PP 2.0 of Professor Paul Wong is introduced. It emphasizes the "need to enhance the positives and manage the negatives in order to increase well-being and decrease mental illnesses" (Wong 2011). This chapter gives an overview of the main terms and definitions of PP as well as its limitations and weaknesses. The tenets of PP 2.0, such as virtue and meaning, are presented. These categories are used to explore the development and changes that occurred throughout the life of V. Frankl, especially during life and work in concentration camps and after the liberation.

In Chap. 5, methodological considerations important to psychobiographical research are discussed, and recommendations to overcome the difficulties inherent in this type of research are suggested. Quality criteria which are important for qualitative research are introduced. Based on the criteria of a "good" psychobiography, the aims and purpose of the study are presented as well as data collection procedures and analysis methods are described.

Chapter 6 presents the results of the biographical data collection of Viktor Frankl's life based on main tenets of PP 2.0 such as virtue and meaning as well as Alexander's indicators of psychological salience and Schultz's prototypical scenes.

In Chap. 7 the results of data collection are discussed in detail to facilitate an understanding of Viktor Frankl's life and to ascertain the effectiveness of Wong's theory in enhancing the positive and managing negative life experiences.

The final chapter draws the study to a close by discussing the conclusions of this research.

1.9 Chapter Conclusion

This introduction presents the structure of the study. It provides an outline of the research to explore and describe the life of Viktor Frankl according to the model of PP 2.0 of Paul Wong (2011, 2020a, b). In the discussion of the results in Chap. 7, aspects of his theory that are congruent with Frankl's life story will be verified. In the following chapter, psychobiographical research is discussed in more detail.

References

Allport, G.W. 1961. *Pattern and growth in personality*. New York, NY: Holt, Rinehart and Winston.
Blanche, M.T., K. Durrheim, and K. Kelly. 2006. First steps in qualitative data analysis. In *Research in practice. Applied methods for the social sciences*, ed. M.T. Blanche, K. Durrheim, and K. Kelly, 320–344. Cape Town: University of Cape Town Press.
Frankl, V.E. 1984. *Man's search for meaning*. New York, NY: Pocket Books.
———. 2000. *Viktor Frankl. Recollections. An autobiography*. Cambridge: Basic Books.
———. 2015. *Es kommt der Tag, da bist du frei*. München: Kösel-Verlag.
Klingberg, H. 2013. *Viktor und Elly Frankl*. Wien: Facultas. WUV.
Krippendorff, K. 2013. *Content analysis: An introduction to its methodology*. Thousand Oaks: Sage.
Längle, A. 2013. *Viktor Frankl: Eine Begegnung*. Wien: facultas.wuv.
Mayer, C.H. 2017. *The life and creative works of Paulo Coelho*. New York: Springer.
Mayer, C.-H., and J.P. Fouché. 2021. Lessons learned from Baruch Spinoza: Shame and faith development in the light of challenges in contemporary society. In *Shame 4.0*, ed. C.-H. Mayer, E. Vanderheiden, and P.T.P. Wong. Cham: Springer.
Mayer, C.H., and Z. Kováry, eds. 2019. *New trends in psychobiography*. New York: Springer.
McAdams, D.P. 1988. Biography, narrative and lives: An introduction. *Journal of Personality* 56: 1–18.
McCullough, M.E., and C.R. Snyder. 2000. Classical source of human strength: Revisiting an old home and building a new one. *Journal of Social and Clinical Psychology* 19: 1–10.
Peterson, C., and M.E.P. Seligman. 2004. *Character strengths and virtues*. Washington, DC: American Psychological Association: Hoffman.
Runyan, W.M. 1988a. *Psychology and historical interpretation*. New York, NY: Oxford University Press.
———. 1988b. A historical and conceptual background to psychohistory. In *Psychology and historical interpretation*, ed. W.M. Runyan, 3–60. New York, NY: Oxford University Press.
Schultz, W.T. 2005a. *Handbook of psychobiography*. Oxford: Oxford University Press.
———. 2005b. Introducing psychobiography. In *Handbook of psychobiography*, ed. W.T. Schultz, 3–18. Oxford: Oxford University Press.
———. 2005c. How to strike psychological pay dirt in biographical data. In *Handbook of psychobiography*, ed. W.T. Schultz, 42–63. Oxford: Oxford University Press.
———. 2005d. How to critically evaluate alternative explanations of life events: The case of Van Gogh's ear. In *Handbook of psychobiography*, ed. W.T. Schultz, 96–103. Oxford: Oxford University Press.
Soggie, N.A. 2016. *Logotherapy: Viktor Frankl, life and work*. Lanham: Rowman and Littlefield.
Van Tongeren, D.R., and S.A. Showalter Van Tongeren. 2020. *The courage to suffer. A new clinical framework for life's greatest crises*. West Conshocken, PA: Templeton Press.

Wong, P.T.P. 2010. Meaning therapy: An integrative and positive existential psychotherapy. *Journal of Contemporary Psychotherapy* 40: 85–94.
———. 2011. Positive psychology 2.0: Towards a balanced interactive model of the good life. *Canadian Psychology/Psychologie Canadienne* 52: 69–81. https://doi.org/10.1037/a0022511.
———. 2019. Second wave positive psychology's (PP 2.0) contribution to counselling psychology, [special issue]. *Counselling Psychology Quarterly*. https://doi.org/10.1080/09515070.2019.1671320.
———. 2020a. The maturing of positive psychology and the emerging PP 2.0: A book review of positive psychology (3rd ed.) by William Compton and Edward Hoffman. *International Journal of Wellbeing* 10 (1): 107–117. https://doi.org/10.5502/ijw.v10i1.885.
———. 2020b. *Made for resilience and happiness: Effective coping with COVID-19 according to Viktor E. Frankl and Paul T. P. Wong*. Toronto: INPM Press.
Yin, R.K. 2003. *Applications of case study research*. Thousand Oaks: Sage.
———. 2014. *Case study research: Design and methods*. Thousand Oaks: Sage.

Chapter 2
Psychobiography: A Theoretical Overview

2.1 Chapter Preview

This chapter provides a brief outline of psychobiography as a theoretical approach. Firstly, it gives a definition and outlines the aims of psychobiography. Secondly, it illuminates the history of its development. Thirdly, it presents the value of psychobiographical case study as well as the contribution of psychobiographical research on the life of Viktor Frankl. The chapter ends with a chapter summary.

2.2 Psychobiography: Definition and Its Aims

Psychobiography is defined as "the intensive life-span study of an individual of historical significance in socio-cultural context using psychological and historiographic research methods and interpreted from established theories of psychology" (Ponterotto 2015, p. 379). Mayer and Kováry (2019) describe psychobiography as a "the systematic application of scientific psychology in the interpretation of life and works of significant people like artists, scientists, philosophers, activists or politicians" [1]. Psychobiography combines "the science of psychology and the art of biography" (Howe 1997, p. 237). The difference between biography and psychology relates to the application of psychological theories in the interpretation of biographical data (Fouché and Van Niekerk 2010).

Psychobiography aims at understanding individual lives, uniqueness of people, and how they function (Schultz 2005b). It is less focused on ascertainable details of life—and more on what those details reveal about a person's inner experience such as motives, coping techniques, goals etc. (Schultz 2017). Psychobiographers aims at answering the question about why people think and act as they do (Schultz 2017). It is concerned with the issues of blind spots of people as well as the subjective truth they believe (Mayer and Kováry 2019).

There are two reasons for doing a psychobiography: "to cogently know another person, and to know ourselves" (Schultz 2005a, b, c, d, p. 4). The psychobiographic analysis produces insights and inspiration for new formal propositions that can be tested against larger groups of people (Schultz 2005a, b, c, d). It means that psychobiographies may serve as a resource for the new psychological theories and hypotheses (Schultz 2005a, b, c, d). Moreover, psychobiography, as a case study, can help to prove or facilitate an existing psychological theory (Mayer 2017). In this study, the psychobiographic research will serve as an instrument which proves or facilitates the theory of PP 2.0 of Paul Wong (2011).

2.3 The History of Psychobiography

According to Kováry (2011), the first pioneering work for psychobiography can be seen in the works of Plutarch, who focused on political and historical figures as well as in the book of Vassari "Lives of the Artists" in 1550. To historical antecedents of psychobiography belong to (a) biography; (b) literature; (c) philosophical school of thought named Lebensphilosophie (Kováry 2011).

The starting point of psychobiography is seen in Freud's Leonardo-essay at the beginning of the twentieth century (Mayer and Kováry 2019). It was concerned with one particular detail in Leonardo's diary, "vulture fantasy" (Kováry 2011). Based on it, Freud created a narrative on Leonardo's sexual development. Later some crucial errors were found out in the Freud's analysis connected with translations. The work was finally criticized because it tended to have a pathograpic focus as well as a focus on a "single cue" (Kováry 2011).

After Freud's initiation, psychobiography was a popular research method among psychoanalysts (Mayer and Kováry 2019). The personalities of artists were widely investigated (Kováry 2011). In the first half of the twentieth century, pathographical aspects still shaped psychobiographical analysis (Mayer and Kováry 2019).

In the 1950th, the opportunities and scientific status of psychobiography were questioned. The psychobiography was criticized for generalizations and overvaluation of the childhood experiences (Kováry 2011). After World War II, researchers began to focus on decontextualized dispositional constructs and their measurement. From the 1930s, new approaches such as personality research, known as personlogy, appeared within a psychobiography (Kováry 2011). The psychobiographic method turned from nomothetic to idiographic research. It formed a "historical-interpretative psychology"—psychodynamic and personological traditions together with narrative psychology (Kováry 2011). Later, the historical-holistic approach was widely criticized and went out of style, leading the psychobiography to the "age of stagnation" for the next few decades (Mayer and Kováry 2019, p. 2).

In the 1980s the historical perspective returned in personality psychology. The reason for it was the success of "narrative turn" in psychobiography and new insights in psychoanalysis and philosophy (Mayer and Kováry 2019). Since then, psychobiography has gained more acceptance by the science of psychology (Mayer and

Kováry 2019). Since the 1980s, the modern psychobiography has become more eclectic theoretically, and its focus has widened. It has become more accurate as it concerns the source of criticism and data handling; it reflects on the process of interpretation, validation and the personal involvement of the psychobiographer (Mayer 2017). In the twenty-first Century, psychobiography is moving forward, developing new theoretical and methodological approaches, including Positive Psychology perspectives, exploring meaning and identity in more depth (Mayer et al. 2021a, b), becoming more diverse in its approach, while becoming more inclusive in terms of the choice of subjects of research (Wegner 2020; Mayer et al. 2021a, b).

2.4 The Value and Contribution of Psychobiographical Case Studies

Anderson (2005) claims that a theorist tends to explore areas which have special meaning for their own life. The conclusions of the developed theory tend to coincide with their personal experience. Therefore, there is a dynamic interaction between the theorist and the theory which should help them to understand themselves better and cope with their challenges. According to Anderson (2005), there are the following advantages of the psychobiographical study of psychologists: a better understanding of psychological theory as the theorist's life provides numerous examples of it; the opportunity of finding out a theorist's blind spots, limitations, and overgeneralizations; the advantage of "demystification" of a theorist, better understanding of his life and actions; benefits to the understanding of psychotherapy and psychological testing; reasonable usage of psychological theories according to a case, as "no psychological thinker can see the whole of personality" [209].

Reading the first- and third-person literature on Viktor Frankl, the researcher convinced herself that Frankl's stance and actions towards overcoming challenges in his own life correspond to his developed theory of meaning (logotherapy). As this psychobiographic research deals with the structure and functioning of meaning as well as virtues which provide that meaning (based on the tenets of PP 2.0), there are the following advantages of this study: first, the reader may gain a better understanding of the concept of meaning in overcoming negative experiences on the example of V. Frankl's life. Secondly, it provides an opportunity of finding limitations and overgeneralizations in Frankl's theory for further research. Thirdly, Viktor Frankl can be better understood in his actions and reasons for developing his theory of meaning.

2.5 Conclusion

This chapter provided the definitions and aims of psychobiographic research. It showed the development of psychobiography from eleventh century until now. Finally, the value and contribution of the psychobiographical research on Viktor Frankl were discussed.

References

Anderson, James William. 2005. The Psychobiographical study of psychologists. In *Handbook of psychobiography*, ed. W.T. Schultz, 203–209. Oxford: Oxford University Press.
Fouché, J.P., and R. van Niekerk. 2010. Academic psychobiography in South Africa: Past, present and future. *South Africa Journal of Psychology* 40 (4): 495–507.
Howe, M.J.A. 1997. Beyond psychobiography: Towards more effective syntheses of psychology and biography. *British Journal of Psychology* 88 (2): 235–248. https://doi.org/10.1111/j.2044-8295.1997.tb02632.x.
Kováry, Z. 2011. Psychobiography as a method. The revival of studying lives. New perspectives in personality and creativity research. *Europe's Journal of Psychology* 7 (4): 339–777.
Mayer, C.H. 2017. *The life and creative works of Paulo Coelho*. New York: Springer.
Mayer, C.H., and Z. Kováry, eds. 2019. *New trends in psychobiography*. New York: Springer.
Mayer, C.-H., J.P. Fouché, and R. van Niekerk. 2021a. Creating a meaningful life: Psychobiographical investigations. Special Issue. *Europe's Journal of Psychology*.
———. 2021b. Servant leadership during the struggle for political freedom: A psychobiography of Albertina Sisulu. In *The Palgrave handbook of servant leadership*, ed. Satinder Dhiman, Gary Roberts, and Larry Spears. New York: Palgrave.
Ponterotto, J.G. 2015. Psychobiography in psychology: Past, present, and future. *Journal of Psychology in Africa* 25: 379–389.
Schultz, W.T. 2005a. *Handbook of psychobiography*. Oxford: Oxford University Press.
———. 2005b. Introducing psychobiography. In *Handbook of psychobiography*, ed. W.T. Schultz, 3–18. Oxford: Oxford University Press.
———. 2005c. How to strike psychological pay dirt in biographical data. In *Handbook of psychobiography*, ed. W.T. Schultz, 42–63. Oxford: Oxford University Press.
———. 2005d. How to critically evaluate alternative explanations of life events: The case of Van Gogh's ear. In *Handbook of psychobiography*, ed. W.T. Schultz, 96–103. Oxford: Oxford University Press.
———. 2017. Psychobiography: Theory and method. American Psychologist, 72(5), 434–445. Retrieved January 15, 2020, from https://williamtoddschultz.files.wordpress.com/2018/12/Psychobiography-AP.pdf
Wegner, B.R. 2020. Psychobiography is trending amongst psychologists. Review of Claude-Hélène Mayer and Zoltan Kovary, eds., New Trends in Psychobiography (Springer Nature Switzerland AG: Springer International Publishing, 2019). *Clio's Psyche* 27 (1): 140–144.
Wong, P.T.P. 2011. Positive psychology 2.0: Towards a balanced interactive model of the good life. *Canadian Psychology/Psychologie Canadienne* 52: 69–81. https://doi.org/10.1037/a0022511.

Chapter 3
Viktor Frankl: Life and Works

3.1 Chapter Preview

This chapter provides an account of biographical information on Viktor Frankl. In the literature, information on Viktor Frankl gives various explanations of his character traits, life choices and scientific ideas. Therefore, this chapter presents not only historical facts, but also interpretations of significant events that shaped his life.

This chapter includes insights regarding biographical "facts" with the analysis of those "facts" (Soggie 2016; Längle 2013; Klingberg 2013; Wong 2020a, b) as well as autobiographical works of Viktor Frankl (1984, 2000, 2015, 2017). These works are integrated to provide complex information on the person from different perspectives.

3.2 Early Years

Frankl was born 26.03.1905 in Vienna, Austria. During this time, Vienna was the seat of the Austro-Hungarian Empire, a bastion of Germanic political power (Soggie 2016).

Viktor Frankl stated that he inherited his personal characteristics from both of his parents (Frankl, 2000). In such a way, Frankl explained the tension between rationality and deep emotions in his personality traits (Frankl 2000). His father, Gabriel, represented a Spartan philosophy, he was "a stoic but occasionally hot-tempered man, personifying justice and love to his family" (Soggie 2016, p. 2). Frankl describes him as being religious but having the capacity for critical thought (Frankl 2000). Frankl recalls that as a child, he always felt a sense of security and safety. This feeling came through the family environment, primarily through his father (Frankl 2000). According to Längle (2013), this experience accompanied Viktor Frankl his whole life. For Frankl, the father was an authority figure who always wanted to enforce his will (Längle 2013). He gave the family and his much younger wife clear guidelines on the conduct of life and the religious attitude (Längle 2013). Such paternal behaviour corresponded to the *Zeitgeist* of this time. Längle (2013) claims that Frankl admired his father and tried to emulate him rather than to rebel against him.

His mother was "kindhearted and deeply pious" (Frankl 2000, p. 22); she gifted Frankl with "a deep wellspring of emotion that he could tap into times of trial" (Soggie 2016, p. 2). Längle (2013) reports that he had never heard other descriptions of the mother except that she was "goodness in person" [17].

During his whole life, Frankl felt strongly connected to his parents and parental home (Längle 2013). This connection highlights some unique features. According to Längle (2013), Frankl's relationship with his parents is to be understood in a religious context. Describing the feelings to his mother, Frankl seems to adore her, not emotionally but rather as a saintly figure, creating an emotionless distance between them: When he thought of her, he wanted to sink to his knees and kiss the hem of her dress (Längle 2013). The same distance is to be noticed in the relationships with the father. They saw each other for the last time when they were both imprisoned in a concentration camp. The final conversation highlights the emotional distance between the two, even at this moment of final farewell (Frankl 2015):

> "Do you want to tell me something else?"
> He says: "No, thanks".
> Me: "Do you want to ask me something else?"
> He: "No, thanks".
> Me: "Do you have any complaints?"
> He: "No, thanks".
> "Are you all right?"
> "Yes". [29–30].

Frankl described his last conversation with a giving of the ampoule morphine as a fulfilment of his doctor's duty (Frankl 2015). Once again, there is no emotional dimension in Frankl's narrative: no word of farewell, tears of pain and grief, neither of his father nor himself (Längle 2013). According to Längle (2013), the content of the memory shows a man who is primarily concerned with a pure personal conscience. Instead of the expected suffering of an ordinary man, he was filled with the feeling of fulfilled duty that he had done everything for the father what he could (Längle 2013). Längle (2013) sees this life event as a traditional understanding of duty that characterizes Frankl's generation. This attitude has also been promoted and demanded by the religious communities.

In 1914–18, during the First World War, Frankls experienced tough economic times. Frankl cared for his family since his childhood. In one case, he stood in line at 3 a.m. to buy potatoes (Frankl 2000). His father, Gabriel, was also forced to beg for bread or to steal food in the fields (Längle 2013). The modest circumstances of Frankl's family influenced Frankl's own lifestyle (Längle 2013). He lived a simple life, which he felt comfortable with and did not think about finances and wealth: it was important to him to have so much money that he did not have to think about

3.2 Early Years

it. Längle (2013) states that although he respected rich people, he was able to deal more comfortably with those who knew hard financial situations and made no claims. Later, this foundational idea becomes the idea of logotherapy: to forget oneself and surrender to a higher value or a task (Längle 2013).

At the age of 4 years, little Viktor Frankl became aware of the fact of the human mortality and meaning of life (Längle 2013). Before falling asleep, he often thought about death and the transitory nature of life, which seemed to him to destroy life's meaning (Frankl 2000, p. 29). As these thoughts happened at such an early age, Längle (2013) suggests that the question of the meaning of life was innate in Frankl.

Frankl's teenage years were "time full of philosophical struggle", which formed later the ideas of logotherapy (Soggie 2016, p. 3).

At school, Frankl described himself as a seeker of knowledge, interested in philosophers and experiments (Soggie 2016, p. 2). His father told him many stories from his own time in medical school. During his childhood and teenage years, Frankl was notable by seeking wisdom for its own sake independent of academic achievement (Soggie 2016). At the age of 9 years, he began to study the works of natural philosophers Wilhelm Oswald and Gustav Theodor Fechner (Längle 2013). He was fascinated with the philosophical and psychological ideas of their works. Frankl was called "The Thinker", as he always asked many questions, wanting to know more and more (Frankl 2000).

Until the junior high, Frankl was on the school honour rolls, but then he began to follow his own interests (Frankl 2000). As a 14-year-schoolboy, he began taking adult evening classes in applied psychology and brought the lessons back to his school classroom for demonstrations (Frankl 2000). In these lectures, Frankl developed the idea that humans should not ask what is a meaning of life, rather life is asking us this question, "What is the meaning of this life?" (Frankl 2000). He argued that it was we ourselves who must answer this question on an everyday basis. Therefore, the primary task of living was to discover meaning.

Another basic idea that teenage Frankl discovered was the notion of ultimate meaning or supra-meaning (Soggie 2016). It implies that the full meaning of a person's existence is beyond the grasp of human understanding (Soggie 2016). Therefore, we cannot comprehend it, but we must have faith in it. (Frankl 2000). Although it may implicate the religiousness of Frankl, according to his own words, he had dispensed with this kind of faith: "As a child I was religious, but then, during puberty, I passed through an atheistic period." (Frankl 2000, p. 57).

At the age of 15 or 16, Frankl broke away from the traditional parental and religious habits of thought and fell into a cognitive-theoretical mode (Längle 2013). At this age, Frankl fell into a psychologistic and sociological "temptation" (Längle 2013). Frankl became a nihilist, his belief in God receded and eventually got lost for some time. It was replaced by scientific faith and a political activity fuelled by a revolutionary belief in the future. Around 1919, Frankl began a correspondence with Sigmund Freud (Längle 2013). He sent him material from his interdisciplinary reading, which he thought could interest him. One of the proudest and thrilling moment for Viktor came when he wrote an article in the park in 1924 about the origin of the mimic movements of affirmation and negation and sent it to Freud, hoping to please him with his work (Frankl 2000). Freud gave positive feedback and sent it for consideration in the International Journal of Psychoanalysis (Frankl 2000).

In the year 1920/1921, 15 years-old Frankl gave his first lecture on the "Meaning of Life" in the philosophical working group of the Viennese adult education centre by Edgar Zilsel (Längle 2013). Later, in 1923, the 18-year-old Frankl published his first article in the Youth supplement of a daily newspaper (Längle 2013).

Viktor Frankl dreamed of becoming a doctor (Soggie 2016). The popularity of Freud influenced Frankl's interest in the psychiatry. At the age of 19, Frankl made two steps toward his dream: he was admitted into medical school and joined Sigmund Freud's Vienna Psychoanalytic Society (Soggie 2016). According to Soggie (2016), "these early experiences, struggles, and goals set the stage for what was to become Viktor's most productive period" [3].

However, Frankl did not stay Freud's supporter for a long time. A decisive endeavour which has contributed to the Frankl's switch to individual psychology was the meeting with the colleague of Siegmund Freud with the aim of Frankl's training analysis and inclusion in the psychoanalytic society (Längle 2013). Frankl arranged a job interview with Federn and appeared on time, as described by Längle (2013), as following: When Frankl was escorted to the study, Federn was sitting behind his desk. Without looking up, he silently motioned Frankl to a chair with a wave of his hand. After a rough time, he asked him: "Well, Mr Frankl, what is your neurosis?". Viktor Frankl answered something about his "anal character" and his "anxious-anankastic features" [46–47]. Later, reflecting on this meeting, he became aware of a double reductionism of Federn's approach. He was embarrassed by Federn's suppression of the human dimension (no greeting, no apology, no explanation) and pathologism, as he was seen by Federn exclusively in his neurosis and not as a human being. According to Pytell (1997), this experience contributed to the fact that Frankl did not apply for training analysis.

Frankl was disappointed with the reductionism of psychoanalysis because it did not satisfy his longing to understand the people (Soggie 2016). However, he found himself increasingly interested in the Individual Psychology of Alfred Adler. "Through Adler's group and his medical studies, Viktor was able to explore other research areas like psychosomatic medicine with mentors Drs. Rudolf Allers and Oswald Schwarz" (Soggie 2016).

In the year 1927, Frankl was expelled from Adler's society because of his "unorthodox views" (Costello 2014). The exclusion from the individual psychology union plunged Frankl into a void and disorientation, which lasted about 10 years (Längle 2013).

After this incident, Viktor Frankl took a break from theoretical pursuits and began focusing on practice aiding in opening several student counselling centres, first in Vienna, and then in six other cities, based on the Vienna model (Frankl 2000). "That was the first in many years when no student suicides were reported in Vienna", wrote Frankl in his autobiographical book (Frankl 2000, p. 68). According to Längle (2013), Frankl wanted to offer help to students and teenagers. Furthermore, he wanted to do the consulting for them for free, because he has learned financial hardship and knew that many young people could not afford such services. This

3.2 Early Years

activity has helped Frankl to recover again despite the massive loss of community (Längle 2013). Moreover, this time enabled him to incubate his theory of meaning (Soggie 2016). He had developed the concept of three groups of values, or three ways to find meaning in life (Soggie 2016, p. 4):

1. a deed we do;
2. an experience we have;
3. an attitude we adopt.

In addition to the youth counselling centres, Frankl founded the magazine "Man in everyday life" (Längle 2013). All this aimed at developing mental-spiritual care of the population in coping with everyday life. Längle (2013) claims that both activities, counselling centres and foundation of the magazine, reveal two of Frankl's main traits: his idealistic activity and social commitment.

Despite the heavy demands of the specialist doctor training as well as volunteer activities in the youth counselling centres and the series of lectures, a feeling of emptiness and disorientation slowly came (Längle 2013). All these activities did not bring real fulfilment to Frankl (Längle 2013). Längle writes that although Frankl was a doctor, he was something else that was not discovered by him at the time. That is what will later become his life's work.

Between the age of 26 and 31 years, he spent time "visiting vaudevilles" (Längle 2013). In his manuscript, he also writes that he enjoyed it very much when he was "batting around in the women's beds" (Längle 2013). However, later he realized that in this way, he just wanted to numb himself. Längle (2013) suspects that Frankl had suffered at the time under apathy and boredom. This condition led him to a sense of meaninglessness. Later, Frankl described it as an "existential vacuum" into which sexual libido proliferates (Längle 2013, pp. 58–59).

Choosing the specialization between obstetrics and dermatology was another struggle for Frankl during his time at the medical school at the University of Vienna (Frankl 2000). However, the friend convinced Viktor Frankl that he had another calling quoting from the philosopher Soren Kierkegaard to make his point: "Do not despair at wanting to become your authentic self" (Frankl 2000, p. 53). This statement greatly affected Frankl, and he decided no longer to avoid his psychiatric self-actualization (Frankl 2000).

Frankl gave various lectures on psychotherapy and philosophy. From 1927 the lectures, addressing the question of meaning, followed regularly. Frankl's emphasis was not so much on the treatment of mental disorders, but on the prophylaxis, the psychohygiene, on the mediation of a human image and a philosophy of life (Längle 2013). This activity proved to be immensely fulfilling. Later, he remembered that teaching classes also had allowed him to meet women, "which he found to be a pleasant side-benefit" (Soggie 2016, p. 4). Once, Frankl used an occasion of his classes "to lure a woman that he has met at the dance" (Soggie 2016, p. 4). He described her one fantastic lecturer, who used to give fascinating lectures (Frankl 2000). Then, he invited her to the lecture hall, where he reserved a place near the front of the class. On settling into her seat, he exclaimed: "One can imagine the impression it would make on a girl as her date suddenly left his seat and, greeted with an audience, step up to the lectern" (Frankl 2000, p. 71.).

After graduating from medical school in the year of 1930, Viktor went on to specialize in general psychiatry and neurology (Soggie 2016). During his residency period at the Steinhof Psychiatric Hospital, Frankl was responsible for the treatment of severely depressed individuals. In his therapy, he found great value in using his sense of humour. Frankl invented the technique of paradoxical intention, which he found useful in everyday situations. He recalls the situation when a police officer stopped him for the traffic violation (Frankl 2000). Frankl began to exaggerate about how being written a ticket was well deserved. The officer reacted by calming Viktor and did not write him a ticket.

In the late 1930s, the Nazi influence was growing within Austria, but the Jewish population of Vienna was hopeful (Soggie 2016). In 1937, Frankl completed his residency and began a short-lived private practice in neurology and psychiatry (Frankl 2000). Frankl recalls one episode of that time during his lecture entitled Nervousness as a Phenomenon of Our Time. The SS man intended to disturb his lecture and force its and (Frankl 2000). Frankl, in turn, firmly decided "to make the impossible possible, and the lecture in such a way that he will forget why he came here" (Frankl 2000, p. 76). He called this act as a "rhetorical bravery" of his life, as the officer just remained at the door (Frankl 2000, p. 76).

By late 1938 Nazi took over all Jewish establishments and forced all Jewish professionals to wear a six-pointed yellow star (Frankl 2000). Frankl was no longer able to run his practice as a Jew. He soon received the post of chief of neurology at a Jewish hospital, called Viennese Rothschild Hospital. He offered him a new position which was expected and hoped to protect Frankl and his parents from deportation (Frankl 2000).

By late 1939, over half of the Jews in Vienna immigrated for safer places. The rest stayed in the city despite the increasingly hostile climate (Jones 1957). At that time, Frankl continued to work as a junior doctor at the neurological department of the Viennese Rothschild Hospital. Frankl continued his medical work and could make some scientific interventions with dying patients (Frankl 2000). Moreover, he even succeeded to publish his scientific article in the Swiss Journal Ars Medici. During these times, because of the catastrophic political situation, up to ten suicide attempts came into the Rothschild clinic every day. Frankl took every effort to save people who attempted suicide. "I do respect the decision of people to end their lives. But I also wish others respect the principle that I have to save lives as long as I am able" (Frankl 2000, p. 79). Frankl believed that saved life, even under the condition of further suffering (because of incurable illness, or deportation to a concentration camp) will serve the ultimate possibility of self-actualization of a person (Frankl 2000).

All doctors in mental hospitals were required by the Nazi regime to identify those with a psychoanalytic disorder or developmental disability in order to slate them to euthanasia (Frankl 2000). Viktor Frankl tried to save as many lives as possible by setting the patients in a Jewish home for senior citizens and certifying patients with schizophrenia as having other disorder. Frankl recalled with sadness the times when he could not save lives.

In September 1939, Viktor Frankl was the only sibling of the Frankl family who remained with his parents in Vienna, supporting them with whatever he could (Soggie 2016). His position at the Rothschild Hospital offered some protection from deportation to the concentration camps for both, him and his parents (Soggie 2016). At this time, he met his future wife Tilly Grosser, a nurse at the hospital. He was thinking about the idea of marrying her, and suddenly one situation brought him to this final decision to marry her (Frankl 2000): Being with his parents during one afternoon, Tilly was preparing the meal. Suddenly, Frankl received a call to perform a brain surgery. Returning home several hours later, he assumed that he had missed his lunch. However, Tilly welcomed him, asking in a caring way about the patient and bringing him lunch that she had saved for him. This simple act made Viktor Frankl take the decision and ask Tilly to marry him, "not because she was this or that. But because she was she." (Frankl 2000, p.86).

In December 1941, he hesitated to immigrate to the USA because of his parents, who needed protection (Frankl 2000). Viktor Frankl would tell the story how he prayed for directions from heaven, and soon after he saw a piece of the tile where stood: "Honour your father and your mother; that your days may be long in the land that God gives you" (Exodus 20:12) (Frankl 2000). So, he decided to stay with his parents to care for them. Längle (2013) reports that this quote served Frankl as a metaphysical justification, a religious foundation, a mandate from God.

In December 1941, Viktor and Tilly Frankl got married being the second last couple at the special office for Jews (Frankl 2000). After the marriage, they lived with Viktor's parents in a small flat (Soggie 2016). When Tilly became pregnant, she was forced to have an abortion, because of the danger to be sent to the concentration camp. Later, Frankl dedicated the book "The Unheard Cry for Meaning" to his lost child (Frankl 2000).

Despite the forced abortion, Frankl hoped that his position at the hospital would protect his family from deportation. However, in late September 1942, the Frankls were called in for deportation. Frankl recalls this time as follows: "But nobody who was not alive in that time can imagine the atmosphere, what it was like. You cannot imagine it!" (Klingberg 2013, p. 33).

The last Jews were aware of what would mean forced deportation into a Jewish ghetto with its inconvenience, and slim-like, uncomfortable conditions (Soggie 2016). However, they hoped that their family and friends would keep the community spirit during the deportation.

3.3 Theresienstadt

In 1942, Frankl and his family were transported to Theresienstadt (Soggie 2016). Frankl had to leave many prized possessions behind, such as the Freud's postcards as well as his written patient case histories (Klingberg 2013).

Viktor, his parents and wife, could not live together in the camp because there were separate living quarters for young, the elderly, women, and men (Soggie 2016).

Tilly was granted a two-year exemption from transfer to Auschwitz (Frankl 2000). Viktor, however, was called to "Transport East" which they assumed meant Auschwitz. Although Tilly was asked by Viktor to stay in the factory in order to avoid more significant danger, she volunteered to go with him and was approved for transport. When men and women were being separated, Frankl recalls telling her "in the firmest tone possible": "Tilly, stay alive at any price. Do you hear? At any price!" (Frankl 2000, p. 90). After his liberation, on his return to Vienna, Viktor learned that Tilly had died with many others after the liberation of Bergen-Belsen by English soldiers.

Later, after arriving at Theresienstadt, Viktor Frankl was selected to stay at a local SS prison (Soggie 2016). Although Viktor Frankl was advised to faint and fall to the ground if he should be ordered to this location, he failed following this advice. Being too proud, he agreed going there thinking he had little to fear (Soggie 2016).

Being in that prison, he had to conduct senseless acts of work, such as throwing water on a compost heap. However, he was not able to satisfy the sadistic wishes of the SS and received a severe beating. Recalling that experiences, Frankl says, "I was brought back to the ghetto with thirty-two injuries. Tilly saw me on the street in Theresienstadt and said, 'Viktor, for heaven sake! What have they done to you?" (Frankl 2000).

After that, Frankl was assigned to special duties as a doctor (Soggie 2016). He was to oversee a group of sick people, which allowed him to see his family every day. Moreover, he used to develop suicide intervention teams. The people on these teams would watch for signs of depression in the barracks and then report potential suicidal cases to Frankl. Due to these efforts, the number of suicides dropped (Soggie 2016).

The position as a doctor enabled Frankl to smuggle a vial of morphine, which he used to relieve his father's sufferings during the last days. In 1943, the father of Viktor Frankl died because of starvation and pneumonia being 81 years old (Längle 2013).

In 1944, Frankl appeared on the list of those being moved to other camps (Soggie 2016). Tilly Frankl volunteered to go with him, although Viktor Frankl was against this decision, as this place could be worst then Theresienstadt (Klingberg 2013). Frankl's 65-years-old mother remained in Theresienstadt (Soggie 2016). Viktor Frankl hoped she would survive by avoiding transport. However, she was also transported to Auschwitz and was murdered in the gas chamber in the 23.10.1944 (Längle 2013).

3.4 Auschwitz

In 1944, Viktor Frankl and his wife were deported to Auschwitz in Poland, to a camp called Birkenau. The conditions were worse than those at Theresienstadt: the camp was overcrowded, and water and sanitation were not enough, resulting in the rapid spread of disease (Soggie 2016). Frankl (2000, p. 93) recalls a "miracle" of the first selection at the railroad station. Dr. Mengele was selecting prisoners into the two queues: the right queue was for labour in the camps, the left queue for the gas chambers. In the case of Viktor, he pointed to the left. Viktor recognized that there is nobody on the left, and as nobody looked, he switched over to the right line. "Only God knows, where I got that idea or found the courage", remembered Frankl later (Frankl 2000, p. 93).

Entering Auschwitz, he was required to discard his coat and take an old, torn one. In the pocket of the coat, he found the leaf, torn from a prayer book. There was written: "Hear, oh Israel, the Lord our God is one" (Frankl 2000). This was a clear sign for Frankl to live what he had espoused before about the meaning of life—to practice what he preached despite all circumstances. Therefore, the harsh life circumstances did not discourage Frankl to develop his theory of life and meaning further. Soggie (2016) describes this process as following:

> Where he had given up the chance to go to the United States to advance his studies, now life itself forced him to live with the problem that he had struggled with in theory. Viktor was testing defeat and discovering meaning in the reality of irrevocable commitments and acts. What he had previously struggled to clarify in theory, in the boundaries of self and outlook, the experience made porous and permeable [13].

In his book, "Man's Search For Meaning" (1984), Frankl describes his observations of the camp life. He distinguished three phases of psychological states of prisoners: the period following prisoner's admission; the period when the prisoner is well entrenched in camp routine; and the period following his release and liberation.

3.4.1 The Phase of Shock

According to Frankl (1984), the symptom that characterizes the first phase was a state of shock. According to Soggie (2016), Viktor was not immune to it, as this phase was overwhelming.

Later, analysing this phase, he came to understand that people use self-deception strategies in order to deal with images of death known as a delusion of reprieve (Frankl 1984). The doomed person desperately grasped for hope in the face of death. Frankl was not an exception, having hope for a better fate than other prisoners (Frankl 1984).

The phase of shock prevailed and became even more profound when he realized that personal achievements meant nothing anymore (Soggie 2016). Once, Frankl tried to take one of the old prisoners into his confidence. He tried to explain to him that he was hiding a great scientific work, his "life's work" (Frankl 1984, p. 32), which should be kept at all costs. The old prisoner grinned, then amused, mocking, insulting, until he bellowed one word at him, a word that was ever-present in the vocabulary of the camp inmates: "Shit!" (Frankl 1984, p. 33). Later, he lost his scientific work. At that moment, he saw the ugly truth and did what marked the culminating point of the first phase of his psychological reaction: he struck out his whole former life. Now he understood who he was: the number 119.104 (Frankl 1984). "What stood behind that number and that life mattered even less: the fate, the history, the name of the man" (Frankl 1984, p. 73).

Although the loss of the book scripture was a painful moment for Frankl, he brought himself to the question: "What kind of life would it be, whose meaning depends entirely on whether a book gets published?" (Frankl 2000, p. 95). So, as an Abraham was prepared to sacrifice his only son, so Frankl was ready to sacrifice his "spiritual child" (Frankl 2000, p. 95). On the other hand, Frankl reported that he had succeeded in surviving the camp's reality with his attempts to reconstruct that lost manuscript (Frankl 2000).

3.4.2 Apathy and Lessons of Survival

The atmosphere of the camp reduced people to law down to their basic instincts. Frankl observed how prisoner's illusions disappeared one by one, and with it, the will to live and survive (Frankl 1984). Being in the second psychological phase, he—as other prisoners—did not fear death anymore. Even the gas chambers were not horrific anymore, as they spared them the act of committing suicide (Frankl 1984). At that time, Frankl could sit and eat his soup, as people walked near him, dragging dead bodies along the floor (Frankl 1984).

Once, Frankl was asked by a chef doctor to take up medical duties in another camp with typhus patients. Against the advice of the friends, Frankl agreed to volunteer (Frankl 1984):

> I knew that in a working party I would die in a short time. But if I had to die, there might at least be some sense in my death. I thought that it would doubtless be more to the purpose to try and help my comrades as a doctor than to vegetate or finally lose my life as the unproductive labourer that I was then [69].

Viktor understood that the adjustment to the camp life was difficult but possible (Frankl 1984). Frankl considered suicide as a way to escape from all the harsh circumstances. However, Frankl realized the danger of such thoughts and decided not to touch the electrically charged fence, which was the prevalent method in the camp to commit suicide.

Despite the apathy, Frankl did not lose his human dignity. Once, Frankl was working on a railway station in a snowstorm (Frankl 1984). He worked hard at mending the track with gravel. For only one moment, he paused to get his breath, and

3.4 Auschwitz

the guard beat him. "The most painful part of beatings is the insult which they imply", recalls Frankl (1984, p. 43).

Viktor Frankl describes apathy as a mechanism of self-defence (Frankl 1984). Although Viktor also reached that level of indifference, there were still joyful moments in his life. Frankl dreamed and imagined his wife (Frankl 1984):

> My mind clung to my wife's image, imagining it with an uncanny acuteness. I heard her answering me, saw her smile, her frank and encouraging look. Real or not, her look was then more luminous than the sun, which was beginning to rise [56–57].

This visualization strategy enabled Viktor to temporary push apathy out of his experience and focus on his hopes. Moreover, it allowed him to operate in a life-affirming state of mind and to develop his will to find the meaning of his life (Frankl 1984):

> I did not know whether my wife was alive, and I had no means of finding out (during all my prison life there was no outgoing or incoming mail); but at that moment it ceased to matter. There was no need for me to know; nothing could touch the strength of my love, my thoughts, and the image of my beloved. Had I known then that my wife was dead, I think that I would still have given myself, undisturbed by that knowledge, to the contemplation of her image, and that my mental conversation with her would have been just as vivid and just as satisfying [58].

Relationships to hold, love and commitment were the key themes for Frankl at that time, which later became integral to logotherapy. Sense of humour was another way, to overcome the destroyed illusions: "When the showers started to run, we all tried very hard to make fun, both about ourselves and about each other. After all, real water did flow from the sprays." (Frankl 1984, pp. 34–35).

Apart from the strange sense of humour, Frankl pointed out another sensation that seized them, so called "cold curiosity" (Frankl 1984, p. 35), or "emotionless attitude" (Soggie 2016, p. 16). It implied giving up old beliefs and learning new truths. He remembers his anxious desire to know what would happen next after standing in the open air, in the chill of late autumn, naked, and wet from the showers (Frankl 1984). His curiosity turned into surprise, because he did not catch a cold. These and other "surprises" showed Frankl how much humans could endure.

The inner life of Viktor Frankl become more intense, so he also experienced the beauty of art, such as camp songs and cabaret (Frankl 1984). Despite the lost hope of life and liberty, he and other prisoners were carried away by nature's beauty, which they had missed for so long (Frankl 1984).

Once, Frankl had an opportunity to be smuggled out from the camp. However, Frankl understood that he, as a doctor was not able to flee in a good conscious, if his patient needed his advice (Frankl 1984). So, he decided to stay in a camp and told his friend that he could not go with him. This decision helped him to feel relieved from the unhappy feelings. Through these conscious experiences, Frankl realized that the power of choice, spiritual freedom and independence could be preserved—even in the most demanding conditions (Frankl 1984):

> And there were always choices to make. Every day, every hour, offered the opportunity to make a decision, a decision which determined whether you would or would not submit to

those powers which threatened to rob you of your very self, your inner freedom; which determined whether or not you would become the plaything of circumstance, renouncing freedom and dignity to become moulded into the form of the typical inmate [86].

3.5 Postwar Years

After liberation, Frankl entered the third psychological phase of concentration camp prisoners: bitterness and loss. In the first evening after release from the concentration camp, he was unable to feel any joy; he had no strength (Frankl 1984). Frankl called the state of the liberated prisoner "depersonalization" which describes a condition of not believing that the new state of being is real und true (Frankl 1984).

Viktor suffered from moral deformity, bitterness and disillusionment, as he tried to return to his former life. Then, he received the news about the death of his wife Tilly, his mother, brother, and his sister-in-law. He reported that finding the acceptance and compassion of others was difficult (Frankl 1984:

> When, on his return, a man found that in many places he was met only with a shrug of the shoulders and with hackneyed phrases, he tended to become bitter and to ask himself why he had gone through all that he had. When he heard the same phrases nearly everywhere—"We did not know about it." and "We, too, have suffered.", then he asked himself: have they really nothing better to say to me? [113].

Once, in Vienna, Frankl met his good old friend, Paul Polak. He told him about the death of his parents, his brother, and Tilly. He burst out into tears and said to him (Frankl 2000):

> Paul, I must tell you, that when all this happens to someone, to be tested in such a way, that it must have some meaning. I have a feeling—and I don't know how else to say it—that something waits for me. That something is expected of me, that I am destined for something [104].

In the urge of Otto Kauders, in 1945, Frankl wrote the third and last draft of "The Doctor and the Soul" and used it to fulfil one of the requirements for becoming a university lecturer. "This was the only thing that seemed worthwhile to me, and I buried myself to work" (Frankl 2000, p. 105). Therefore, Frankl tried to resolve his soul collapse by writing the book. Längle (2013) reports that works that he created during these years constitute the basis of his scientific life's work.

The books "The Doctor and the Soul" and "Man's Search For Meaning" (originally published as "Nevertheless, Say 'Yes' to Life: A Psychologist Experiences the Concentration Camp") were released in 1946 (Längle 2013). Frankl deliberately chose a provocative title for the book "The doctor and the Soul" as he wanted to emphasize that the doctor has to care for his soul despite any religious affiliation. The book was recognized in 1948 as a habilitation thesis, as Kauders proposed in 1945 (Längle 2013). Three days after its publication, the book was sold out. Numerous other editions followed. An American commission called "The Doctor and The

3.5 Postwar Years

Soul" worthy of translating and it was published in English as early as 1946 (Längle 2013).

In the same year, Frankl dictated "Man's Search For Meaning". First, he wanted to publish it anonymously so that he could express himself freely (Längle 2013). The book was already in print when Frankl's friends convinced him to release it under his name. Frankl reports, he could not refuse the appeal of his friends for courage and accepting responsibility. However, the first edition was released without his name as the cover was already being printed. Initially, the sale of the book was slow. After the translation of the book into English, based on the recommendation of Gordon Allport, the book became more popular. Within 6 years, the book counted 14 editions and more than nine million copies appeared in the USA by 1995 (Längle 2013).

Frankl (2000) says, he had never dreamed that these two books would find such a reception all over the world. The writing process was not easy for him (Längle 2013). The necessity to reprocess his suffering did not motivate him. Writing the books meant a sacrifice for him as he was forced to set aside what he passionately liked, climbing and hiking. Längle (2013) suggests that a higher purpose, the idea of a calling, and the voice of conscience to accomplish a task motivated Frank to write and finish the books.

Frankl reports that writing many other books became the personally satisfying endeavour for him (Frankl 2000), although he suffered under perfectionism and extreme accuracy (Längle 2013). Längle (2013) reports that he could spend hours on single formulations wrote some pages ten times until the formulations were precise.

In 1946, during a visit to his neurological department at the Vienna Polyclinic, Frankl became acquainted with a young nurse who had been sent to him from another department with a request for a guest bed. A year later, she became his wife: Eleonore Katharina Schwindt. His second wife, Elly, supported him in writing his books (Frankl 2000). She had to share the sacrifices with him, perhaps even raise more significant sacrifices then he, "self-denial", as Frankl said (Längle 2013, p. 80). Frankl writes about her: "She is the counterpart to me, both quantitatively and qualitatively. What I accomplish with my brain, she fulfils with her heart." (Frankl 2000, p. 111).

In 1949, Frankl became a father for the first time and only once (Längle 2013, p. 90). In the year of her birth, Frankl dedicated the book "The unconditional human being—Metaclinical Lectures" to his daughter Gabriele (Frankl 2000).

In 1954, Frankl was invited to Argentina for a lecture series on logotherapy (Längle 2013). It was his first longer stay abroad and on the occasion of this conference, the world's first Society for Logotherapy was founded in Buenos Aires (Frankl 2000). However, there was another side to his success: Frankl had many opponents, especially in the Jewish community, since Frankl opposed the thesis of collective guilt (Längle 2013). He advocated, wrote and published a humane ideal of human responsibility, and personally advocated for it by protecting people. It was by no means popular after the war to oppose collective guilt. He even did this in a lecture in which the commander of the French occupation troops was present (Längle 2013). He reported, for example, about a camp leader, an SS man whom he had met and who secretly provided medicine for camp inmates from his own money.

Since Frankl's lectures and books were also very successful in the USA, Frankl was invited to the United States repeatedly (Längle 2013). He began a tremendous lecturing activity, which made him in the 1960's to a popular speaker, first, in English-speaking foreign countries and finally worldwide. He undertook a onehundred lectures tour through America alone; four of them went around the world. There were eventually more than 200 universities outside Europe at which Frankl held lectures. Increasingly, prominent figures from politics and science invited him, such as Pope Paul VI (Längle 2013).

In 1970, Frankl became a professor of logotherapy at the United States International University of San Diego in California (Längle 2013). By 1980, Frankl received three honorary doctorates—a number that few academics achieve. In the late 1980s, he received 25 other honorary doctorates, for a total of 28. So, Frankl was the most decorated scientists with honorary doctorates as a psychiatrist and psychotherapist worldwide. In July 1996, Frankl gave his last interview in front of a broad specialist audience on the occasion of the 1st World Congress for Psychotherapy in Vienna (Längle 2013). The same year he gave his last lecture in which he only spoke for about 20 min (Längle 2013).

In the last months of his life, his heart significantly worsened (Längle 2013). The physicians confronted him with the decision to either undertake a risky operation or likely to quickly be faced with a high risk of heart failure. Frankl opted for surgery during which he died, on 2.09.1997. The next day he was buried with only his closest friends and relatives present. Frankl refused an official funeral and a grave of honour that he would have been granted as an honorary citizen of the city of Vienna. His wish was to lie in the family grave (Längle 2013).

His death triggered a flood of recognition and obituaries (Längle 2013). In almost all German-language newspapers was reported about Frankl's death. On television, it was the top story on the evening news.

3.6 Chapter Summary

This chapter presents the major events in the life of Viktor Frankl according to first- and third-person documents used. This chapter presents the life of Viktor Frankl, his character traits, the birth of his scientific ideas which shaped his life decisions and became a base for the logotherapy. In the findings section, Viktor Frankl's biography will be analyzed, using the theory of Paul Wong (2011), Alexander's and Schultz' indicators and the information described above.

The findings will focus on selected works of Viktor Frankl: "Recollections" (2000) as the first autobiographical manuscript of Viktor Frankl, "The Man's Search For Meaning" (1984) as his classic and most famous logotherapeutic work, as well as private letters from the book "Es kommt der Tag, da bist du frei" ("There will come a day when you are free") (Frankl 2015), which provides in-depth insight into the feelings and life decisions of Viktor Frankl in the post-war-years.

References

Costello, S.J. 2014, February 17. 1923–1927: *From individual psychology to logotherapy (Frankl, Viktor) – Prof Alexander Batthyany*. Dr. Stephen Costello. Retrieved January 15, 2020, from https://drstephenjcostello.wordpress.com/2014/02/17/1923-1927-from-individual-psychology-to-logotherapy-frankl-viktor-dr-stephen-costello

Frankl, V.E. 1984. *Man's search for meaning*. New York, NY: Pocket Books.

———. 2000. *Viktor Frankl. Recollections. An autobiography*. Cambridge: Basic Books.

———. 2015. *Es kommt der Tag, da bist du frei*. München: Kösel-Verlag.

———. 2017. *Wer ein Warum zum Leben hat*. Bad Langensalza: Belz Verlag.

Jones, E. 1957. *The life and work of Sigmund Freud*. New York: Basic Books.

Klingberg, H. 2013. *Viktor und Elly Frankl*. Wien: Facultas. WUV.

Längle, A. 2013. *Viktor Frankl: Eine Begegnung*. Wien: facultas.wuv.

Pytell, T. 1997. Was nicht in seinen Büchern steht. Bemerkungen zur Autobiographie Viktor Frankls. *Zeitschrift Für Psychoanalyse und Gesellschaftskritik* 39 (2): 95–121.

Soggie, N.A. 2016. *Logotherapy: Viktor Frankl, life and work*. Lanham: Rowman and Littlefield.

Wong, P.T.P. 2011. Positive psychology 2.0: Towards a balanced interactive model of the good life. *Canadian Psychology/Psychologie Canadienne* 52: 69–81. https://doi.org/10.1037/a0022511.

———. 2020a. The maturing of positive psychology and the emerging PP 2.0: A book review of positive psychology (3rd ed.) by William Compton and Edward Hoffman. *International Journal of Wellbeing* 10 (1): 107–117. https://doi.org/10.5502/ijw.v10i1.885.

———. 2020b. *Made for resilience and happiness: Effective coping with COVID-19 according to Viktor E. Frankl and Paul T. P. Wong*. Toronto: INPM Press.

Chapter 4
Positive Psychology 2.0 of Paul Wong

4.1 Chapter Preview

This chapter presents Wong's (2011, 2019, 2020a, b) theory of PP2.0. It emphasizes the need to increase the positives and manage the negatives in order to improve well-being and reduce mental illnesses (Wong 2011). Compared to classical positive psychology, PP2.0 emphasizes the need to notice and synthesize not just positive, but also negative outcomes (Wong 2019, 2020a, b). It takes a stance on the imperative of virtues as well as shifts the focus from individual happiness and success to a meaning-centred approach to making life better for all people (Wong 2011). There are four tenets of PP2.0: virtues, meaning, resilience and well-being. Because of the focus of this study and its space limitations, the researchers analyse selected aspects, namely the virtues of transcendence and the structure of meaning in the life of Viktor Frankl only. These two tenets are presented below.

4.2 The Principles of Positive Psychology 2.0

PP can be seen as the scientific study of positives experiences and positive individual traits as well as its development (Peterson and Seligman 2004). It deals with fostering positive emotions and building a new character which can also directly or indirectly alleviate suffering and to undo its root causes (Nolen-Hoeksema et al. 2005).

According to Wong (2011), the mission of PP2.0 is to give the answers to what makes life worth living and how to improve life for all people. Although the classical Positive Psychology is concerned with the question of how to deal with negative experiences through the development of positive traits, Wong (2011) claims that it offers to concentrate only on the positive effects and potentials of life. Therefore, it has not provided a comprehensive answer to the question of what to do with negative emotions and experiences. Moreover, too much emphasis on positive effects and potentials can be counterproductive for human development because such negative states as guilt, regret, anger or frustration can also serve as motivation for a good change.

Wong (2011) suggests a balanced model of PP2.0, where both sides, positive and negative experiences as well as strengths and weaknesses of people are integrated. Such an approach enables us to understand the complexity of life in its totality. In order to achieve this, Wong suggests a comprehensive new taxonomy that recognizes the legitimacy of negatives in all subdomains of PP2.0. According to PP 2.0, the most effective strategy to maximize the positive and minimize the negative is to discover benefits or potentials of negative traits and negative outcomes. Acceptance of suffering and enhancement of happiness should not be regarded as two different goals (as it was in classical Positive Psychology), but as interdependent endeavours. According to Wong (2011, 2019, 2020a), the mission of PP2.0 is to embrace the dark side of human existence, as well as the necessary another half of the circle of happiness and wellbeing. Therefore, the new science of flourishing through suffering is to study how people navigate between negative and positive emotions. Resilience and sustainable happiness result from overcoming adversities and achieving an optimal balance between positive and negative events and experiences (Wong 2020b; Wong and Worth 2017). In the following chapter, two of the four pillars of PP 2.0 are presented in-depth.

4.3 Central Tenets of Positive Psychology 2.0

Wong (2011) provides the Four Pillars of PP2.0, such as virtue, meaning, resilience and well-being. This study uses the pillars of virtue and meaning in order to describe the life of Viktor Frankl. In the following, these two pillars will be described and explained in detail.

4.3.1 Virtues

According to Peterson and Seligman (2004), the primary purpose of PP is to encourage the development of human strengths and civil virtues. The strength should be "morally valued in its own right", and the person's display of it should not diminish other people (Peterson and Seligman, 2004, p. 17). According to McCullough and Snyder (2000), virtue is a "psychological process that consistently enables a person to think and act so as to yield benefits to him or herself and society" [1]. Peterson and Seligman (2004) distinguish six broad categories of virtues: wisdom, courage, humanity, justice, temperance, and transcendence. These six categories are made up of 26 character strengths which define every virtue more precisely (Peterson and Seligman 2004).

4.3 Central Tenets of Positive Psychology 2.0

In this study, the virtue of transcendence is chosen based on numerous reasons for the analysis: Firstly, transcendent experiences and optimal human functioning seem to be interconnected (James 1999 [1902] in Mayer and May 2019, p. 157). Therefore, the researcher aims at answering the question of how the transcendent virtue may contribute to the optimal human functioning if the person experiences negative life events on the scale of Viktor Frankl's life. Secondly, the virtue of transcendence provides the person with meaning (Peterson and Seligman 2004) which was the central component of Frankl's approach to overcoming suffering and retaining the will to live. Thus, the researcher suggests that cultivation of transcendent virtue is crucial in the meaning-making process and the development of resiliency towards negative life events and suffering. In the following, the virtue of transcendence is explained in detail.

4.3.2 The Virtue of Transcendence

The virtue of transcendence is defined as "strengths that forge connections to the larger universe and provide meaning" (Peterson and Seligman 2004, p. 30). Peterson and Seligman (2004) separate transcendence from religiosity, as transcendent does not need to be sacred or connected to spiritual or religious practices. Thus, "transcendence can be something or someone earthly that inspires awe, hope, or even gratitude" (Peterson and Seligman 2004, p. 39). The virtue of transcendence includes the following character strengths:

- *Appreciation of beauty* refers to the "ability to find, recognize, and take pleasure in the existence of goodness in the psychological and social worlds" (Peterson and Seligman 2004, p. 537). The emotional experience of awe or wonder is the defining feature of this character strength (Peterson and Seligman 2004).
- *Gratitude* means "a sense of thankfulness and joy in response to receiving a gift, whether the gift is to be a tangible benefit from a specific other or a moment of peaceful evoked by natural beauty" (Peterson and Seligman 2004, p. 554).
- *Hope* represents a cognitive, emotional, and motivational stance toward the future resulting in expecting the best and working to achieve it; "believing that a good future is something that can be brought about" (Peterson and Seligman 2004, p. 30).
- *Humour* is defined as (a) "playful recognition, enjoyment, and/or creation of incongruity", (b) "a composed and cheerful view on adversity that allows one to see its light side and thereby sustain a good mood", (c) "the ability to make others smile and laugh" (Peterson and Seligman 2004, p. 584).
- *Spirituality* refers to "having coherent beliefs about the higher purpose and meaning of the universe; knowing where one fits within the larger scheme; having beliefs about the meaning of life that shape conduct and provide comfort" (Peterson and Seligman 2004, p. 30). The spiritual beliefs are "persuasive, pervasive and stable. They influence the attributions people make, the meanings

they construct, and the ways they conduct relationships" (Peterson and Seligman 2004, p. 600).

These character strengths will be used in order to analyze the development of the transcendent virtue in the life of Viktor Frankl.

4.3.3 Meaning

Hoffman (2009) concludes that "the attainment of meaning is one of the most central aspects of human existence and necessary to address in existential therapy" [49]. Positive psychologists consider meaning as one of the components of happiness and the good life (Peterson and Seligman 2004; Wong 2015).

In order to explain the structure and functions of meaning, Wong (2012) suggests the PURE-Model which stands for Purpose, Understanding, Responsible Action and Enjoyment. In the following, the PURE-Modell of Wong will be explained in detail:

- *Purpose* stands for the overall direction, life goals, and core values, providing the framework of daily deliberations and decisions. Purpose also includes existential values and questions about what matters in life. It includes the devotional to something higher than oneself. The purpose is concerned with the following questions: "What does life demand of me? What should I do with my life? What matters in life? What is the point of working so hard?" (Wong 2012, p. 10).
- *Understanding* stands for a sense of self-identity, and how the world works, the pursuit of self-understanding and self-knowledge (Wong 2012). A sense of coherence includes enlightenment about life and death and one's place in the larger scheme of things (Wong 2012). Understanding entails self-reflection and self-acceptance, which are components of a meaningful life (Wong 2012). Concerning constructivist psychology, Wong claims that that understanding requires the meaning-making process (Wong 2012). This process is based on personal history and an idiographic way to experience the world (Wong 2012). Moreover, meaning-seeking and making are shaped by culture, language and ongoing relationships (Wong 2012). The process of understanding is concerned with the following questions: "What's happened? Why isn't it working? What does this mean? What I am doing here? Who I am? Why did he do that? What does he want?" (Wong 2012, p. 10).
- *Responsible action* is concerned with appropriate reactions and actions (Wong 2012). Good decisions are ethical, lead to successful or satisfying results and contribute to the well-being of others (Wong 2012). Responsible action asks the following questions: "What is my responsibility in this situation? What is the right thing to do? What options do I have? What choices should I make?" (Wong 2012, p. 11).
- *Enjoyment and evaluation* are the last components of the PURE-Model of Paul Wong. According to Wong (2011), positive feelings are inevitable from doing the good, considering one's highest purpose and best understanding. Even if the

decision or action fails, one can feel satisfied with it (Wong 2011.). If it does not happen, the person has to reevaluate the purpose and understand actions in order to do midcourse corrections and not to remain stuck in a rut (Wong 2011). Therefore, discontent serves as a positive function when it motivates the person to positive changes (Wong 2011). At this stage, the person asks themselves the following question: "Have I achieved what I set out to do? Am I happy with how I lived my life? If this is love, why am I still unhappy?" (Wong 2012, p. 11).

These components of meaning are used to analyze the structure of the meaning-making process in the life of Viktor Frankl.

4.4 The Need for Positive Psychology in the Context of Psychobiography

Traditionally, psychobiography is anchored in the theoretical realm of psychoanalysis and psychoanalytic theories (Elms 1994, 2007; Mayer and Kováry 2019; Schultz 2005a, b, c, d). However, PP is gaining interest in the context of modern psychobiographies (Mayer 2017; Mayer and May, 2019, pp. 156–157). It is useful in psychobiographical research and in establishing new insights and models to health and well-being in individuals across the lifespan (Mayer and Kováry 2019).

The focus on PP in psychobiography is needed for several reasons: Firstly, it provides new orientation from a psychological, spiritual and societal perspective as they provide orientation taking into consideration global changes, insecurity, disorientation and unhealthy developments (Mayer and May 2019). Secondly, the PP perspectives provide a perspective shift from psychoanalytic, critical and pathological views to positive views on the individual's life (Mayer and May 2019). Therefore, other individuals can be encouraged to seek meaningfulness through the psychobiographical explanation of other outstanding persons from the light of PP and find positive role models (Mayer and May 2019). Thirdly, PP2.0 can use the psychobiographic method in order to explain on real-life examples how to use, regard and confront negative emotions, suffering and stress in order to survive and even flourish as a person (Mayer and May 2019).

4.5 Conclusion

This chapter provided information on the principles of PP 2.0. The two out of four relevant tents of PP 2.0, which are relevant for this psychobiographic research are provided. The need for PP in psychobiography is explained and strengthened.

According to PP 2.0 of Wong (2011), the focus on only the positive is no longer defensible, because positives and negatives are connected and appear as dualities. Therefore, the dialectic, rather than binary principle is more applicable to the reality of human experiences. As the life of most people is hard and full of suffering, the pursuit of happiness and experience of suffering should not be regarded as mutually excluding factors. PP2.0 emphasizes that the person needs to confront the dark side of human existence in order to achieve authentic happiness and resilience. The perspectives of PP can be used in psychobiography in order to establish new positive insights on human functioning from a psychological, spiritual, societal and health perspective and provide people with positive role models. Moreover, a psychobiography can make the approaches of PP more understandable for a wider audience as the person can gain a deeper understanding about dealing with negative life aspects based on the examples of extraordinary real live scenarios.

References

Elms, A.C. 1994. *Uncovering lives: The uneasy alliance of biography and psychology*. New York, NY: Oxford University Press.

———. 2007. Psychobiography and case study methods. In *Handbook of research methods in personality psychology*, ed. R.W. Robbins, R. Fraley, and R.F. Krueger, 97–113. New York, NY: Guilford Press.

Hoffman, L., M. Yang, F.J. Kaklauskas, and A. Chan. 2009. *Existential psychology east-west*, 1–67. Colorado Springs, CO: University of the Rockies Press.

James, W. 1999. *The varieties of religious experience. A study of human nature*. New York: Modern Library. (original Work published 1902).

Mayer, C.H. 2017. *The life and creative works of Paulo Coelho*. New York: Springer.

Mayer, C.H., and Z. Kováry, eds. 2019. *New trends in psychobiography*. New York: Springer.

Mayer, C.H., and M. May. 2019. The positive psychology movements PP1.0 and PP2.0 in psychobiography. In *New trends in psychobiography*, ed. C.H. Mayer and Z. Kováry, 155–171. New York: Springer.

McCullough, M.E., and C.R. Snyder. 2000. Classical source of human strength: Revisiting an old home and building a new one. *Journal of Social and Clinical Psychology* 19: 1–10.

Nolen-Hoeksema, S., T. Widiger, and T.D. Cannon. 2005. *Annual review of clinical psychology, Vol. 1: Annual reviews*. https://doi.org/10.1146/annurev.clinpsy.1.102803.144154.

Peterson, C., and M.E.P. Seligman. 2004. *Character strengths and virtues*. Washington, DC: American Psychological Association: Hoffman.

Schultz, W.T. 2005a. *Handbook of psychobiography*. Oxford: Oxford University Press.

———. 2005b. Introducing psychobiography. In *Handbook of psychobiography*, ed. W.T. Schultz, 3–18. Oxford: Oxford University Press.

———. 2005c. How to strike psychological pay dirt in biographical data. In *Handbook of psychobiography*, ed. W.T. Schultz, 42–63. Oxford: Oxford University Press.

———. 2005d. How to critically evaluate alternative explanations of life events: The case of Van Gogh's ear. In *Handbook of psychobiography*, ed. W.T. Schultz, 96–103. Oxford: Oxford University Press.

Wong, P.T.P. 2011. Positive psychology 2.0: Towards a balanced interactive model of the good life. *Canadian Psychology/Psychologie Canadienne* 52: 69–81. https://doi.org/10.1037/a0022511.

———. 2012. Toward a dual-system model of what makes life Worth living. In *The human quest for meaning. Theories, research and applications*, ed. P.T.P. Wong, 3–22. New York, NY: Routledge.

———. 2015. *Integrative meaning therapy: From Logotherapy to existential positive interventions | Dr. Paul Wong*. Retrieved January 15, 2020, from http://www.drpaulwong.com/integrative-meaning-therapy

———. 2019. Second wave positive psychology's (PP 2.0) contribution to counselling psychology, [special issue]. *Counselling Psychology Quarterly*. https://doi.org/10.1080/09515070.2019.1671320.

———. 2020a. The maturing of positive psychology and the emerging PP 2.0: A book review of positive psychology (3rd ed.) by William Compton and Edward Hoffman. *International Journal of Wellbeing* 10 (1): 107–117. https://doi.org/10.5502/ijw.v10i1.885.

———. 2020b. *Made for resilience and happiness: Effective coping with COVID-19 according to Viktor E. Frankl and Paul T. P. Wong*. Toronto: INPM Press.

Wong, P.T.P., and P. Worth. 2017. The deep-and-wide hypothesis in giftedness and creativity [Special issue]. *Psychology and Education* 54 (3/4).

Chapter 5
Research Design and Methodology

5.1 Chapter Preview

In this chapter, the research design and process are introduced. The data collection process is presented, including the sampling procedure and the selection of first- and third-person documents. The process of data analysis and interpretation is described including the content analysis, Alexander's (in Schultz 2005c) indicators of psychological saliency and Schultz's (2005c) keys to identifying "prototypical scenes". Markers of good psychobiographical research are defined and presented. In the end, a chapter summary is provided.

5.2 The Research Design and Process in Psychobiography

The study uses an explanatory and descriptive psychobiographical case study design (Elms 2007) that is qualitative in nature. The following key principles according to Elms (2007) are used in the process of this psychobiographical research: (a) choosing the subject of research; (b) formulating tentative hypotheses, (c) data collection process including various forms of data collection, (d) revision of the hypothesis, (e) focused data collection (including similarities and contradictions), (f) formulating conclusions. This research process, suggested by Elms (2007), is followed in this psychobiography on Viktor Frankl. However, the research process is not followed in purely chronological order, as described by Elms, but rather combined with the process of data collection, analysis, interpretation and reporting, in a flexible order, as common in contemporary research (see also McAdams 2020), described in the following section.

5.3 Data Collection

The first step in the data collection process in psychobiographical research is the decision on the choice of the subject (Mayer 2017). The subject of this study is Viktor Frankl, a holocaust survivor and a founder of the meaning therapy who was born in 1905. The motivation for the choice of this person for psychobiographical research is described in Sect. 1.7.

This research offers an opportunity not only to understand Viktor Frankl's life, but also to explore how the character strengths of transcendent virtues (see Sect. 4.3.2) influenced Frankl's actions, life choices and imbued his life with meaning. Moreover, the research offers the opportunity to understand the structure and functions of meaning in Frankl's life (see Sect. 4.3.3) and how it supported him to find the will to live and overcome adversities and life challenges.

The research provides the reader with time to focus on an in-depth, new perspective on Viktor Frankl's life, which describes, interprets and reconstructs it. No research could be found that aims at explaining Viktor Frankl's life from a psychobiographical perspective.

In this study, the following first-person documents were used: "Viktor Frankl. Recollections. An autobiography" (Frankl 2000), "Man's Search For Meaning" (Frankl 1984), private letters of Viktor Frankl from the book "Es kommt der Tag, da bist du frei" ("There will come a day when you are free") (Frankl 2015); "Wer ein Warum zum Leben hat" (Frankl 2017).

Concerning third-person documents, the following resources were used in the data collection process: Längle, Alfried (2013) "Viktor Frankl: Eine Begegnung" ("Viktor Frankl: An Encounter"); Soggie, Neil A. (2016) "Logotherapy. Viktor Frankl, Life and Work".

5.4 Data Analysis and Interpretation

In this research, the approach of Kelly (2006) was used in the process of data analysis and interpretation. According to Kelly (2006), the interpretation in the qualitative data analysis needs the cooperation of two approaches: 'insider', or 'first-person' perspective and 'outsider', or 'third-person' perspective. The first approach suggests empathetic context-bound research which aims at developing an understanding of the subjective experience (Kelly 2006), The second one is more experience-distant and is marked by distanciation (Ricoeur 1979). It suggests that the understanding of the context from the perspective of being in the context (empathy) is limited (Kelly 2006). Therefore, the researcher takes into consideration other contextual factors such as history, theory, society, language, politics, e.g. in order to gain new insights from the text.

5.4.1 Content Analysis

In this study, the researcher used the content analysis in order to reduce text and find out relevant information while applying a subjective sense-making. According to Krippendorff (2013), "content analysis is a research technique for making replicable and valid inferences from texts (or other meaningful matter) to the contexts of their use" [24]. In this study, content analysis was used to make replicable and valid inferences about the personality of Viktor Frankl, applying the pre-defined categories from the psychological theory of Paul Wong (2011). Content analysis was also used to identify Alexander's primary indicators of psychological salience (see Schultz 2005c) and Schultz's "prototypical scenes" (Schultz 2005c) in the life of Viktor Frankl. In this research, the content analysis was held due to following steps according to Kelly (2006) and Blanche et al. (2006):

- *Familiarization* and *Immersion* include thorough working the texts (first- and third-person documents on the subject), making notes, drawing diagrams and brainstorming. At this stage, the researcher became familiar with the text, to the point of knowing where necessary quotations occur in it and got to know the overall meaning and the different types of meaning in the texts.
- *Inducing Themes*: the pre-defined themes deriving from the theory of Wong (2011), such as virtue and meaning, were applied to analyze the data in-depth and reduce the data's complexity. While the themes were induced, the researcher, however, tried to move beyond summarizing and generalizing content and applied an open mind in order to find out possible tensions and contradictions in the texts. In order to highlight unusual and important life events, Alexander's primary indicators of psychological salience and Schultz's "prototypical scenes" were also applied in this step.
- *Coding*: in this step, words, phrases, lines, sentences or paragraphs were broken down into labelled, meaningful pieces according to pre-defined categories. The body of material was coded in order to cluster the 'bits' of coded material together under the code heading and further analyze them as a cluster.
- *Elaboration*: in this step, codes were analyzed and interpreted according to the theoretical background. Similarities and contradictions were found out, which should lead to new insights, uniformities and patterns.
- *Interpretation and Checking*: the final step within the content analysis included interpretation using thematic categories from the analysis as subheadings. In this phase, the researcher's interpretations were put together, and possible contradictions and misinterpretations were removed.

5.4.2 Alexander's Indicators of Psychological Saliency

The following section provides a review on Alexander's (see Schultz 2005c) indicators of psychological saliency which were invented to find out the psychological pay dirt through any set of biographical data. There are the following pointers of primary psychological saliency according to Alexander:

- *Frequency* or repetition of any communications, themes, scenes, events, relationship patterns. Repetition can have not only textual or literal form but be also symbolic.
- *Primacy* or what comes first in a text may provide information about something significant, especially in autobiographical writing.
- *Emphasis* as an effort of a subject to accentuate a happening in the form of over-, under-, or misplaced emphasis.
- *Isolation* is an issue which does not fit in the surrounding context. The task of psychobiographer is to "restore the link between the isolated fragment and the web of unconscious ideas for which it stands" (Schultz 2005a, b, c, d, p. 46).
- *Uniqueness* implies unprecedented or especially singular material.
- *Incompletion* means not finished story without conclusion or omitted necessary details. This indicator may evidence things the subject would prefer not to think about or have to do, or whose content provoke guilt or anxiety.
- *Error, distortion, omission*, and *negation*, which may indicate unconsciously driven motives or reasons.

5.4.3 Schultz's Prototypical Scenes

Schultz's keys to identifying the "prototypical scenes" are the tool to identifying a single scene, "supersaliency", influencing and encapsulating the whole life pathway of a person "because of the richness and range of information it condenses." (Schultz 2005c, p. 49). He calls it "prototypical", because it serves as an outline or a model for a whole life. Schultz (2005c) emphasizes that "not all salient scenes rise to prototypical status" [49]. Although prototypical scenes can be identified due to markers provided by Alexander, some of the prototypical scenes, however, may not possess any of them.

Schultz (2005c) provides the following elements of prototypical scenes:

- *Vividness* and *specificity* of recalled story, high emotional intensity due to emphasized colours, carefully positioned characters, detailed dialogues.
- *Interpenetration* which implies the connection of the story with different contexts, activities or human products. Not only the subject tells others about the scene repetitively, but "the scene works its way into a range of psychological or artistic settings, either overtly or allusively" (Schultz 2005c, p. 49).
- *Implication on the "decisive encounter"* between a person and conflict which may result in a developmental crisis.
- Direct or indirect *implication on the family conflict*.
- *Thrownness* which implies that the subject finds themselves in the entirely new anomalous or surprising situation that violates the status quo. Therefore, the

subject has no more the feeling for equilibrium as "old ways of making sense of things do not suffice" (Schultz 2005c, p. 49).

According to Schultz (Schultz 2005c), each life contains one prototypical scene, which serves as a summary of self. Prototypical scenes can be both, positive and negative (traumatic), but the main element is thrownness, as "these scenes depict a contrast, an affront and confrontation with recalcitrant reality" [49]. Nevertheless, not every prototypical scene contains every element above.

According to Schultz (2005c), after finding salient extractions, the researcher should put them into units, "a number of consecutive sentences that form an entity through shared content, microscopic stories with an introduction, an action, and an outcome fragments, whose story life is somehow disturbed" [60].

5.5 Good Psychobiography Markers

In order to understand the "truth" from the available data about the research subject, Schultz (2005a, b, c, d) offers the following criteria of good psychobiographic research:

- *Cogency*, or interpretative persuasiveness: psychobiography must persuade leaving the reader with the feeling of "won over".
- *Narrative structure*: conclusions must "follow naturally from an array of data".
- *Comprehensiveness*: a psychobiography offers a wide range of clarified reasons.
- *Data convergence*: a psychobiographic study should provide more arguments supporting a fact or interpretation.
- *Sudden coherence*: the initially incoherent facts should become cohere elucidating a mystery.
- *Logical soundness*: no logical inconstancies or self-contradictions should be introduced during psychological research.
- *Consistency*: the researcher uses the full range of available evidence as well as general knowledge of human functioning.
- *Viability*: withdrawal from falsifications.

As actions have multiple causes and meanings, complementary explanations are necessary for good psychobiographical research (Runyan 2005). The advantage of multiple explanations is that they provide the interpretation from different perspectives as they depict different aspects of the episode (Runyan 2005). Therefore, multiple psychological theories and different psychobiographical approaches may be applied for one subject in order to provide a multidimensional view on the life of a person.

5.6 Chapter Summary

This chapter presented the research design and process of psychobiographic research on Viktor Frankl. The data collection process was presented. The approaches within the data analysis and interpretation, including the content analysis, Alexander's indicators of psychological saliency and Schultz's keys to identifying "prototypical scenes" were described. Additionally, the markers of good psychobiography research were presented.

References

Blanche, M.T., K. Durrheim, and K. Kelly. 2006. First steps in qualitative data analysis. In *Research in practice. Applied methods for the social sciences*, ed. M.T. Blanche, K. Durrheim, and K. Kelly, 320–344. Cape Town: University of Cape Town Press.
Elms, A.C. 2007. Psychobiography and case study methods. In *Handbook of research methods in personality psychology*, ed. R.W. Robbins, R. Fraley, and R.F. Krueger, 97–113. New York, NY: Guilford Press.
Frankl, V.E. 1984. *Man's search for meaning*. New York, NY: Pocket Books.
———. 2000. *Viktor Frankl. Recollections. An autobiography*. Cambridge: Basic Books.
———. 2015. *Es kommt der Tag, da bist du frei*. München: Kösel-Verlag.
———. 2017. *Wer ein Warum zum Leben hat*. Bad Langensalza: Belz Verlag.
Kelly, K. 2006. Lived experience and interpretation: The balancing act in the qualitative analysis. In *Research in practice: Applied methods for the social sciences*, ed. M.T. Blanche, M.J.T. Blanche, K. Durrheim, and D. Painter, 345–369. Cape Town: University of Cape Town Press.
Krippendorff, K. 2013. *Content analysis: An introduction to its methodology*. Thousand Oaks: Sage.
Längle, A. 2013. *Viktor Frankl: Eine Begegnung*. Wien: facultas.wuv.
Mayer, C.H. 2017. *The life and creative works of Paulo Coelho*. New York: Springer.
McAdams, D.P. 2020. *The strange case of Donald J. Trump: A psychological reckoning*. Oxford: Oxford University Press.
Ricoeur, P. 1979. The model of the text: Meaningful action considered as a text. In *Interpretive social science: A reader*, ed. P. Rabinow and W.M. Sullivan. Berkley: University of California Press.
Runyan, W.M. 2005. How to critically evaluate alternative explanations of life events. In *Handbook of psychobiography*, ed. W.T. Schultz, 96–103. Oxford: Oxford University Press.
Schultz, W.T. 2005a. *Handbook of psychobiography*. Oxford: Oxford University Press.
———. 2005b. Introducing psychobiography. In *Handbook of psychobiography*, ed. W.T. Schultz, 3–18. Oxford: Oxford University Press.
———. 2005c. How to strike psychological pay dirt in biographical data. In *Handbook of psychobiography*, ed. W.T. Schultz, 42–63. Oxford: Oxford University Press.
———. 2005d. How to critically evaluate alternative explanations of life events: The case of Van Gogh's ear. In *Handbook of psychobiography*, ed. W.T. Schultz, 96–103. Oxford: Oxford University Press.
Soggie, N.A. 2016. *Logotherapy: Viktor Frankl, life and work*. Lanham: Rowman and Littlefield.
Wong, P.T.P. 2011. Positive psychology 2.0: Towards a balanced interactive model of the good life. *Canadian Psychology/Psychologie Canadienne* 52: 69–81. https://doi.org/10.1037/a0022511.

Chapter 6
Research Findings on Viktor Frankl's Life

6.1 Chapter Preview

In this chapter, the life of Viktor Frankl is reconstructed through content analysis based on the two tenets of the model of PP2.0 (Sects. 4.3.2 and 4.3.3) such as virtue and meaning. Since the term virtue is extensive, this research deals only with the character strengths of transcendent virtues such as appreciation of beauty, gratitude, hope, humour, spirituality. Paul Wong's PURE model (2012) is used to analyze the structure of meaning in Viktor Frankl's life. Transcendent virtues, as well as the structure of meaning, will be analyzed during the different stages of Viktor Frankl's life. Alexander's indicators of psychological saliency as well as Schultz's prototypical scenes were used to interpret key aspects of Frankl's autobiographical book "The Man's Search For Meaning" as well as to get a more in-depth insight into a personality of Viktor Frankl.

6.2 The Virtue of Transcendence

The virtue of transcendence is viewed as "strengths that forge connections to the larger universe and provide meaning" (Peterson and Seligman 2004, p. 30) in Sect. 4.3.2. It is used to analyze how the character strengths of this virtue, such as appreciation of beauty, gratitude, hope, humour and spirituality, may be crucial in finding meaning and overcoming life difficulties and adversities.

6.2.1 Childhood and Youth

Appreciation of Beauty
There were no examples found for this code during childhood and youth period in Viktor Frankl's life.

Gratitude
There were no examples found for this code during childhood and youth period in Viktor Frankl's life.

Hope
There were no examples found for this code during childhood and youth period in Viktor Frankl's life.

Humour
One example of humorous events from childhood is found out in an analyzed material. Frankl told his mother, how he came to understand the medicine:

> One picks out people who want to take their lives anyway and happen to be sick. You give them all sorts of things to eat and drink—such as shoe polish or gasoline. If they survive, you have discovered the new medicine for their sickness! (Frankl 2000, p. 29).

It is striking that already in the childhood years Frankl thought about the types of medicine that he would use in his future professional life. Probably, already at an early age, Frankl thought about becoming a doctor. This fact has been influenced by his father, who wanted to study medicine but dropped out because of financial reasons (Frankl 2000). It is also noticeable that already at an early age, Frankl thought about survival despite every circumstance. In the future, the concept of survival in spite of prevailing conditions will be the core point in his theory of meaning (logotherapy).

Spirituality
Regarding his religiousness and faith, Frankl wrote that as a child, he was religious (Frankl 2000). Frankl described his mother as a person of a kind soul and a pious heart (Längle 2013). According to Längle (2013), the original description of his mother was "kindhearted and pious spirit" [17]. Both names are often used in a religious context. They imply an emotional connection as well as an appreciative and respectful treatment of the son towards his mother. In his work, Längle (2013) wrote that he never heard anything from Frankl about his mother other than "She was kindness in person" [17]. It can be assumed that Frankl's relationship with his mother included a religious aspect and was shaped by the etiquette of those times towards the parents.

Frankl's father is described by him as an opposite of the mother: spartan and frugal, but not stingy (Längle 2013). He also was described as being dutiful and having rigid principles (Längle 2013). Frankl remembers how his father "forced" him and his brother Walter to read the prayer correctly in Hebrew (Längle 2013, pp. 23–24). They could get the ten hellers if they could read the text without errors (Längle 2013). However, that only happened a couple of times a year (Längle 2013).

It can be concluded that the father was also a religious person who strictly followed his principles and rules.

During the puberty, Frankl passed through an atheistic period (Frankl 2000), which was shaped by scientific faith and political activity (Längle 2013). However, this period did not last long. Therefore, the researcher concludes that religiousness of Frankl took its roots from the parental home. Frankl might have developed his faith and connection to God on different levels. Emotionally, due to mother's warmth and support; and rationally, due to religious practices which his father carried out (such as a regular reading of the Bible).

6.2.2 Before the Concentration Camps

Appreciation of Beauty

In his autobiography, Frankl stated that he was impressed by the beauty of his first wife Tilly, but the real deciding factor was "her natural intuition, her understanding heart" (Frankl 2000, p.85). Once, Frankl was excited by the reaction of Tilly after some good news from the Jewish Community Service, asking Tilly's mother to start a new job (Frankl 2000). She exclaimed: "Well, isn't God something!" (Frankl 2000, p. 86). Frankl described it as "the most beautiful and certainly the shortest summa theologiae (to speak with Thomas Aquinas)" he ever had heard (Frankl 2000, p. 86). Therefore not "visible" things or achievements but rather, intelligence, positive character traits and good deeds were regarded by him as beautiful and highly appreciated.

Gratitude

There were no examples found for this code during adolescent years in Viktor Frankl's life.

Hope

Frankl (2015) described his experience of hope on the example of giving the lecture and being interrupted by the arrival of the SA-man. He decided to proceed to speak in order to do his best to make him stay and listen to him (Frankl 2015). He achieved his goal. Frankl wrote: "So you see, what is possible if you believe in the possibility" (Frankl 2015, p. 28). In this example, Frankl's hope empowered him to undertake risky steps. The feeling of hope made him active and helped overcome fear giving strength to complete the task despite the challenging situation.

Humour

Frankl described himself as a humorous person. In his book "Viktor Frankl. Recollections. An Autobiography" he gave various examples of jokes and bon mots he made during his professional and private life:

- During the opening lecture at the "Styrian Autumn" festival in Graz:

  [...] I wanted to indicate that I was qualified to speak both as medical man and as a philosopher, yet I wanted to play down the fact that I had a doctorate in each field. So, I said: "Ladies and gentlemen, I have both medical and philosophy doctorates, but usually I do not mention this. Knowing my dear colleagues in Vienna, I expect that instead of saying Frankl is twice a doctor, they would say he is only half a physician (Frankl 2000, p. 38).

- During a lecture in Munich replying to the answer, how can a busy professor have time for healthy sex life, or even know much about it:

  "You know, my friend", I replied, "your words remind me of an old Viennese joke. A man greets a baker and hears that he has ten children. He asks him, 'Tell me, when do you have time to bake?'". The audience laughed. (Frankl 2000, p. 38).

- In the theological school of an American university, answering the question about Paul Tillich's concept of the "the God above God":

  I had never heard of the concept but answered calmly: "If I answer your question regarding 'the God above God' it would imply that I consider myself a Tillich above Tillich" (Frankl 2000, p. 38).

- After the Frankl's wedding ceremony when he walked with Tilly and past a bookstore that showed in its window a book with a title, "We want to Get Married":

  After a long hesitation, we dared to enter, Tilly still in her veil, and both of us wearing the yellow Jewish stars. I got a kick out of making her ask for the book. I wanted to encourage her self-assertion. And so, there she stood: white veil, yellow star on her dress, and in response to the salesclerk's question about what she would like, she said with a blush: "We Want to Get Married" (Frankl 2000, p. 87).

Frankl used jokes in order to promptly respond to the questions during his lectures relaxing the atmosphere and keeping the interest of his audience. He also tended to make jokes in his private life which might have helped him to keep the positive atmosphere in the family and distance from negative feelings.

Spirituality

Frankl wrote that he did not like confessing his faith in the frame of his logotherapeutic methods and techniques as a psychiatrist. He thought that this would not serve the spreading of his scientific ideas (Frankl 2000). However, in his book "Viktor Frankl. Recollections. An Autobiography", Frankl described his behaviour, and decisions which seem to be strongly shaped by his faith and religiousness:

- Attitude toward setbacks. Frankl describes his attitude toward setbacks as following: "I kneel down in my imagination and pray that nothing worse will happen to me in the future" (Frankl 2000, p. 36).
- Attitude toward parents. Viktor Frankl decided to stay with his parents in Vienna and let his visa to the USA lapse, although it might have meant his deportation the

6.2 The Virtue of Transcendence

concentration camp and possible death. This decision was influenced by the words of his father who cited words from the Bible: "Honor thy father and thy mother, that thy days may be long upon the land which the Lord thy God giveth thee" (Frankl 2000, p. 83).
- The decision to live according to the principles of the logotherapy, after he coincidentally found out a scrap of paper in his coat in a concentration camp, where the principal prayer of Judaism, the Shema Israel ("Hear, oh Israel, the Lord our God is One") was written down (Frankl 2000, p. 94).
- Readiness to sacrifice the most important intention, a publication of his book which he called his "spiritual child". This decision was compared by Frankl with a history of Abraham in the Hebrew Bible, who was ready to sacrifice his son in order to fulfil the will of God (Frankl 2000).
- Asking his mother for a blessing before being transported to Auschwitz (Frankl 2015).

These examples show the link between Frankl's faith and his decisions, life choices and attitude toward challenges. The researcher suggests that Frankl's belief helped him to deal with a fear of death and danger staying bold in his principles and not to give up in difficult circumstances.

6.2.3 During the Concentration Camps

Appreciation of Beauty
The first description concerning the awareness of beauty was found out in the book "Viktor Frankl. Recollections. An Autobiography" when he was deported to the camp Auschwitz. He described the contrast between severe pain and tortures he experienced in the morning and beauty of the jazz in the evening "with all its contradictions of beauty and hideousness, humanity and inhumanity" (Frankl 2000, p. 93). It is striking that despite great suffering and fear, Frankl still was able to notice and reflect on beauty even in Auschwitz. This ability seems to have enabled Frankl to be aware of the present moment, which is crucial for finding and preserving life meaning (Pattakos 2010).

In his book "Man's Search For Meaning", Frankl mentioned the beauty of nature. Contemplating it, Frankl wrote that he often thought about his wife Tilly and her appearance (Frankl 1984). He imagined her "with an uncanny acuteness" (Frankl 1984). For Frankl "her look was then more luminous than the sun which was beginning to rise" (Frankl 1984, pp. 56–57). Frankl described these experiences emotionally and detailly compared to other descriptions of his experiences. However, it is striking, that Frankl started to write about Tilly too late in his book although she might have served him as a reason and motivation to survive in the camp. The researcher suggests that the reason for that lays in the character traits of Viktor Frankl who tended to be more rational but still was able to experience deep feelings. Moreover, the researcher suggests that the rational mindset of Frankl, as well as his belief to the own theory of meaning, might have enabled him to direct and explain his strong emotions in the context of his logotherapeutic ideas. Therefore, the feeling of longing to Tilly was instrumentalized in the context of logotherapy. It helped Frankl to find and keep the meaning of life in the hostile surroundings of the camp and direct his emotions. The researcher assumes that the recollections of Tilly were brought late in the book as Frankl aimed primarily to explain his logotherapeutic ideas and after that, rationally depict his feelings.

Frankl also mentioned cabaret and music gatherings in the camp which helped a few ordinary prisoners to forget their fatigue even though they missed their daily portion of food by going there (Frankl 1984). However, Frankl did not say if this case was also true to him. Frankl distanced himself from this experience describing other prisoners but not his own experience.

The examples above show that despite suffering Frankl still was able to notice and enjoy the beauty of nature and art in the camp. These moments enabled him to forget his suffering and dream about things which brought the sense of joy and happiness. However, Frankl did not show the readers his deep "irrational" emotional experiences or his weaknesses. Instead, Frankl interpreted his feelings and emotions from the viewpoint of logotherapy.

Gratitude

According to Frankl, the prisoners were grateful for every mercy happened to them: time to delouse before going to bed, an opportunity to sleep and not be awake in the night (Frankl 1984). The researcher did not find out what Frankl personally was grateful for. However, the researcher suggests that there were still some reasons to be grateful, which Frankl omitted to describe in his book. As an example, an opportunity to work as a doctor according to his professional field, being able to save some lives due to logotherapeutic sessions in a camp etc. Instead of showing the reader the feeling of gratitude, Frankl described emotionlessly his efforts to help their comrades.

Hope

After transportation to the camp, Frankl as other prisoners hoped that they would be reprieved and that the camp reality would not be so hostile as they were told (Frankl 1984). Talking with other prisoners about the death, Frankl estimated his chances to survive at about one in twenty. However, he also told them that he had no intention to give up because "for no man knew what the future would bring, much less the next hour" (Frankl 1984, p. 103). Therefore, Frankl had hope for a better destiny.

Being in the concentration camp in the Auschwitz, Frankl repeatedly thought about the feature trying to distance himself from the circumstances that surrounded him. In his book "Recollections. An Autobiography", he described the situation when he was hardly able to bear the hunger, the cold and the pain of his frozen and festering feet (Frankl 2000). He described his situation as "bleak, even hopeless" (Frankl 2000, p. 98). However, in that times he used to imagine that he stood at the lectern "at the lectern in a large, beautiful, warm and bright hall" (Frankl 2000, p. 98). In his imaginary lecture, he was reporting about his experiences in the camp. Later, these hopes came true (Frankl 2000). Therefore, conscious hope for the better future enabled Viktor Frankl to stay bold in his intention to be resistant toward the present challenges in a concentration camp. However, Frankl wrote that his and other prisoner's hope had not stayed long. When the hope has been lost, the prisoners were overwhelmed by a sense of bitter sarcasm toward the reality (see below) (Frankl 1984).

Humour

After gradual loose of all illusions and hopes, Frankl reported that the prisoners were overcome by a grim sense of humour because they felt that they had nothing to lose except their "so ridiculously naked lives" (Frankl 1984, pp. 34–35). The researcher suggests that sarcasm enabled Frankl and other prisoners to distance from their bitter feelings and weaken their anger. According to Pattakos (2010), humour was meaningful because it helped the prisoners forget their horrific situation, even if only for a moment. "Humour was another of the soul's weapons in the fight for self-preservation." (Frankl 1984, p. 63).

Spirituality

Describing the camp life, Frankl referred to the inner value of a human, which is anchored in higher and more spiritual things and cannot be shaken by the camp life (Frankl 1984). He also calls it human liberty, which means spiritual freedom in reaction to any given surroundings (Frankl 1984).

Being in a concentration camp, Frankl came to his knowledge of the highest goal which human can aspire—love (Frankl 1984). Thinking about his wife, he came to his knowledge that "love goes very far beyond the physical person of the beloved. It finds its deepest meaning in his spiritual being, his inner self. Whether or not he is actually present, whether or not he is still alive at all, ceases somehow to be of importance" (Frankl 1984, p. 104). Again, Frankl's love toward his wife is depicted in the context of logotherapy which highlights the priority of a higher purpose. This higher purpose is spiritual, invisible and not entirely comprehensible for humans. Therefore, Frankl described his love, not emotionally but rather cognitively. His description of love seems to be transcendent and emotionally distanced. Therefore, by re-understanding of love as independence from the physical presence of the beloved, Frank might have stayed resilient towards his fear of Tilly's death and loss of his motivation to survive.

6.2.4 After the Concentration Camps

Appreciation of Beauty

There were no examples found for this code in the period after concentration camp in Viktor Frankl's life.

Gratitude

In his letters, Frankl wrote that he was grateful for every moment of his life because "everything is not so important to what we have experienced" (Frankl 2015, p. 43).

He wrote that he had been grateful for every joy and for a chance to work according to abilities and inclinations (Frankl 2015). The moments of gratitude were present in Frankl's letter before he got to know about the death of his wife Tilly.

Hope

After being released from the concentration camp Auschwitz, Frankl hoped that everybody out of his family members was alive. However, he had a fear of the moment of certainty (Frankl 2015). After he got to know that his mother and the wife had not survived, he had lost his sense of life meaning (Frankl 2015). During this period there were found no more positive remarks regarding hope to the better future in Frankl's letters and books. Frankl seemed to get in a crisis.

The only exception is found out in Frankl's letter to Wilhelm and Stepha Börner, in which he expressed hope that his book "The Doctor and the Soul" would be published soon so that he finally had this "mental delivery" behind him (Frankl 2015, p. 40). Despite the deep disappointment, Frankl had the hope towards his life task as a doctor and an author. The concept of meaning was replaced by the wish to fulfil his duty, namely publish his book.

After the book became popular, the narrative of hope and faith occurred in Frankl's letters again. At that time, he also met his future second wife, Eleonore Katharina Schwindt. Therefore, after finding out about Tilly's death, Frankl experienced the crisis as his life meaning seemed to get lost. However, his wish to fulfil his duty and publish his book "The Doctor and the Soul" gave him strength for work. After meeting Elly Schwindt and the success of his book, Frankl got his sense for meaning again, which can be visible from his letters which will be described below.

Humour

Humour and wits came up in Frankl's letters after getting to know Elly Schwindt and success of his book "The Doctor and the Soul". Frankl used to write ironical and humorous letters to his sister Stella to Austria. One of the examples is a letter to his sister with the request to send him her photographs, otherwise, he would not recognize her (Frankl 2015). Alternatively, the humorous letter which was written by both Eleonore and Viktor Frankl:

> You know, Stella, all day I had to admire Viki, he was not a bit excited and pretended that marrying was something every day like brushing one's teeth (Letter to Stella Bondy, Frankl's sister, written together with his second wife Eleonore Frankl) (Frankl 2015, pp. 88–89).

Spirituality

As mentioned before, Frankl's hope for a better future with his wife Tilly was destroyed. At that time, he experienced deep disappointment, loneliness and futility. However, Frankl seemed to reestablish his will to live through his faith.

In his letter to Gustav and Ferdinand Grosser, he wrote that he regarded God as the only power to hold his inner world together (Frankl 2015). He believed in God as the only way to find consolation: "There is no consolation anymore. The only thing left is to go through the Bible from time to time" (Frankl 2015, p. 55). Frankl seems to have overcome his meaning crisis through his faith by reading the Bible and fulfilling his duty—writing the book "The Doctor and the Soul".

The success of his book "The Doctor and the Soul" and his popularity, was again linked by Frankl with God and his grace (Frankl 2015). He also writes: "The 1000 wonders of God, which allowed me to survive as one of a very few comrades, have shown me the grace of being able to complete the book now" (Frankl 2015, pp. 59). It is noticeable that Frankl regarded the success of his book not as his own but rather as a present of God who directed his ways.

Being in Vienna, Frankl missed his sister who lived in Australia. He linked his hope to see her again with the will of God: "Dear Stellerl—if you knew how often I was dreaming of you all these years! And now the Lord God has added that there is hope that I can hug you in the foreseeable future!" (Frankl 2015, p. 63). Linking his wishes with the will of God, Frankl might have stayed resilient toward every outcome, even if it did not fit his expectations. The stance of humility and trust to God enabled Frankl not to be worried about the future as he believed that God would arrange everything: "So I am not worried, and you do not need to be worried about me. "Just be always cheerful—God will help you on", said the blessed dad (recently on the transport to Theresienstadt)" (Frankl 2015, pp. 73–74).

6.3 Meaning

This section deals with the question of meaning in the life of Viktor Frankl. Using the PURE-Modell of Paul Wong (see Sect. 4.3.3), the researcher aims at answering the question of how the meaning was created, lived through action and evaluated by Viktor Frankl.

6.3.1 Before the Concentration Camps

Purpose
Already at the age of 15 or 16, Frankl developed his understanding of the meaning in life which shaped his life choices, core values and life direction. Frankl claimed that people should not ask for the meaning of life, "since it is we who are being asked" (Frankl 2000). Therefore, the person should take responsibility for their existence and answer this question on their own (Frankl 2000).

In his early age, Frankl developed the idea of ultimate meaning, or suprameaning, which remains beyond a person's comprehension. According to Frankl, the person should believe that their existence served an ultimate meaning despite any difficulties and life challenges (Frankl 2000). Frankl believed that the suprameaning could not be comprehended; therefore, the person could have only faith in it (Frankl 2000).

At the age of 24, Frankl developed the concept three possible ways to find meaning in life (1) a deed person does, a work they create; (2) an experience, a human encounters, love; and (3) a change of attitude toward that fate, when confronted with an unchangeable fate (Frankl 2000). Therefore, Frankl formulated his theoretical understanding of the concept of meaning at the age of 15. He believed that the person should answer the question of life on their own believing that human existence serves a higher goal which cannot be perceived by a human. He found out three ways of finding meaning: deeds, experience, or love and change of attitude. These notions influenced his daily deliberations and decisions throughout his whole life which will be explained below.

Understanding

As a child, Frankl often thought about death, and if the transitory nature of life might destroy its meaning (Frankl 2000). He often asked himself about the meaning of his own life and day (Frankl 2000). Viktor Frankl came to the conviction that every life situation contained "the seed of meaning" (Frankl 2000). In his book "Recollections. An Autobiography", he reported the he was able to see the meaning beyond every miserable situation, and "to turn an apparently meaningless suffering into a genuine human achievement" (Frankl 2000, p. 53). He was convinced that the meaning in life can help even the person with a hard illness to overcome their suffering and actualize themselves.

Therefore, already at a young age, Frankl reflected on the meaning of life and death. He concluded that every negative situation has its purpose and meaning. The researcher suggests that Frankl's understanding of his life and role in a larger scheme of things was also shaped by his faith and religiousness which provided him with a sense of purpose and meaning (more details in Sect. 6.2).

Responsible Action

The following actions and decision based on the understanding of the purpose in life and consequences on other people are described by Viktor Frankl in his book "Recollections. An Autobiography":

- The idea of self-actualization by choosing to study psychiatry instead of dermatology or obstetrics (Frankl 2000).
- The concept of meaning despite suffering: Frankl believed that the essentials of logotherapy should have saved his sense of meaning. Therefore, he decided to write the first draft of the book "The Doctor and the Soul" before his deportation (Frankl 2000).
- The concept of meaningful deeds: Frankl offered lectures without honorarium when he was convinced that a lecture might have been relevant to an audience (Frankl 2000).
- Faith, religiousness: Viktor Frankl decided not to fly to the USA and stay with his parents in Vienna. This decision resulted from the "hint from heaven" (Frankl 2000) when Frankl's father cited a passage from the Bible.

Therefore, Frankl's core values and daily deliberations (see purpose) as well as his understanding of the meaning of life and death (see meaning) had a direct impact on his actions.

Enjoyment and Evaluation

Talking about the significance of unconditional meaning orientation, Frankl wrote that the people were receptive to his words. He experienced himself being "clay in the potter's hand" (Frankl 2000, pp. 55–56). Frankl seems to have enjoyed working as a lecturer and a doctor talking about the meaning and purpose of life.

6.3.2 During the Concentration Camps

Purpose

Being deported to Auschwitz, Frankl pursued his logotherapeutic ideas developed in Vienna. He was convinced of the ultimate meaning of life despite every suffering. These notions shaped his interpretation and understanding of the camp life, suffering and death during the camp life. Being in a concentration camp, Frankl developed his already existing ideas. He regarded suffering as a way to achieve something, turning negative experiences to a human triumph (Frankl 1984). Frankl's ideas of meaning became deeper during his time in a concentration camp. These ideas bear spiritual or even religious character: transcendent love as the ultimate goal, meaning of sacrifice, spiritual freedom to choose behaviour and reaction to every situation.

Understanding

Observing other prisoners, Frankl noticed that their problem was if they would survive because only then their suffering would have meaning for them. For Frankl, the main question was, however, reverse: he asked himself if the suffering and dying make sense (Frankl 2015). He came to the conviction that for him the life is to be worth experiencing if it is provided with unconditional meaning and not "the mercy of the rawest coincidence—namely, chance" (Frankl 2015, p. 18). Therefore, outer conditions, suffering and danger of death did not diminish Frank's motivation to stay resilient and aim to overcome the challenges of camp life. The hope to see his wife Tilly served for Frankl as another reason to stay alive.

Responsible Action

Frankl followed his belief of unconditional meaning and worth of life despite every suffering, which resulted in the following actions:

- The will to survive despite any circumstances: as a doctor, he knew that if he fell asleep or became unconscious during the night, there will be a cardiovascular collapse. Therefore, he has tried to keep awake artificially in order to survive (Frankl 1984).
- Readiness to accept reality, sacrifice the most important and be humble: After the loss of his manuscript for the book "The Doctor and the Soul" Frankl experienced great inner pain. However, he decided to bring himself to be ready to sacrifice his book, a kind of "a spiritual child" for him, as Abraham was prepared to sacrifice his only son, "in order to be judged worthy of its eventual publication" (Frankl

2015, p. 33). In his letters, he reported that he also had used the time in the camp Türkheim to reconstruct the book (Frankl 2015).
- The idea of transcendent love, and a good deed for others: he tried to help his comrades as a doctor in order to be a proactive labourer and not to "vegetate" (Frankl 1984, pp. 69, 102–103).
- Hope for a better future: he tried to distract himself from thinking trivial things. Instead of it, he practised turning his thoughts to a better life imaging himself as a lecturer in front of an attentive audience. Frankl reported that by this method, he succeeded in rising above the situation and the sufferings of the moment (Frankl 1984).

Enjoyment and Evaluation

Frankl regarded his decision to stay with his parents and not to emigrate to the USA as a decision which corresponded to the value of "the will to meaning" and of self-transcendence—the reaching out for something beyond person's own interests (Frankl 1984). After providing his father with pain-relieving medicine and being with him in the last minute of his life, Frankl wrote about the feeling of absolute satisfaction. He was happy: "I had done mine, and I had achieved that I could be with my father until the last moment of consciousness" (Frankl 2015, p. 30). Therefore, Frankl was convinced that life and actions might become meaningful in a larger scheme of things if the person decides to pursue not their own interest but aims at helping and supporting others despite any danger.

6.3.3 After the Concentration Camps

Purpose

After Frankl learned that his mother was murdered in Auschwitz and his first wife Tilly had died in Bergen-Belsen, his life's meaning got lost (Frankl 2015). He no longer spoke of his survival as mercy, but rather as a burden. He neither feared nor desired his death, but he had the feeling that he had "nothing to look for" (Frankl 2015, p. 51). In one of his letters, Frankl wrote the following: "Who has no analogous fate, cannot understand me tired, unspeakably sad, unspeakably lonely, I have nothing to hope for and nothing to fear anymore, I have no joy in life anymore, only duties, I live out my conscience ..." (Frankl 2015, p. 48).

The idea of life meaning resulting from hopes about a better future seems to get in crisis, but Frankl still tried to find reasons not to give up and live according to his moral values conscience.

At those times, Frankl seemed to re-understand his life purpose and meaning. He wrote that he was aware of the task of his intellectual work, logotherapy and existential analysis, and the writing of his book, "The Doctor and the Soul", which he had already begun to write before the deportation (Frankl 201). Therefore, not hope but duty and obligation became meaningful for Frankl: "Nothing has remained—accept the responsibility for the spiritual work that I have to fulfil—

still and despite, or: perhaps also because I have to suffer so much" (Frankl 2015, p. 13).

Understanding
In his letter to Paul Polak, Frankl wrote that he felt the deep meaning beyond all the suffering he experienced: "Paul, I must tell you, that when all this happens to someone, to be tested in such a way, that it must have some meaning. I have a feeling—and I do not know how else to say it—that I am destined for something" (Frankl 1984, p. 104). Believing in the meaningfulness of his experiences, Frankl became resilient and could deal more efficiently with the negative emotions resulting from the death of his mother and wife.

Viktor Frankl wrote that he also felt a kind of a shame, deep disappointment and bitterness on being allowed to breathe, while other gorgeous people and many of his friends had died (Frankl 2015). Frankl wrote that this shame created for him a distance to all happiness and suffering of the earth (Frankl 2015). However, Frankl used that feeling of shame as a motivation to do something meaningful and important: "it makes you feel that you are only worthy of the grace of life if you are leading something" (Frankl 2015, p. 43).

On the other hand, Frankl emphasized that he did not withdraw from his affirmation of life, even when he experienced disappointment, sadness and grief: "I increasingly realize that life is so infinitely meaningful, that even in suffering and even in failure there must still be meaning" (Frankl 2015, p. 49).

Responsible Action
The following decisions and actions resulting from Frank's life goals, core values (see purpose) as well as his view on life and death (see understanding) were found out in the literature:

- Making choices according to own conscience: after the liberation from concentration camps, Frankl worked as a doctor in the hospital for Displaced Persons in Bad Wörishofen. In order to look for his mother and wife Tilly, he quoted his job and left the "good conditions" (Frankl 2015, p. 44). Frankl understood that that decision would not be appreciated by his boss. However, his priority was living with a good conscience (Frankl 2015).
- Faith and practising religion: For Frankl, it was a great concern to care for the grave of his 16-year-old patient, who died in his department before his deportation to the concentration camps. The girl was baptized Catholic. On this occasion, Frankl wrote a letter to the pastor of the Roman Catholic Church with a request to have a funeral mass read for that girl (Frankl 2015).
- Conducting his "duty" as an author of books and a lecturer: Between 1945 and 1949, Frankl published eight books. He also held numerous lectures and radio languages at home and abroad (Frankl 2015). On behalf of Otto Kauders, Frankl wrote the third and last draft of "The Doctor and the Soul" and used it to fulfil one of the requirements for becoming a university lecturer. In case of repetition of the history, Frankl was preparing to emigrate to Australia with his second wife

Eleanore and daughter Gabriele. Frankl asked his sister Stella to set up a notary archive for his books and publications in Australia (Frankl 2015).

Enjoyment and Evaluation

Frankl wrote that he could not leave his parents alone during the war in Europe. So, he stayed with them and finally was also sent to the concentration camp. He did not regret his decision. It was a matter of responsibility for him (Frankl 2015). Frankl wrote to his sister in Australia that he considered it to be a mercy that he had a good conscience after giving support and a little joy to his parents according to his "humane, modest forces" (Frankl 2015, p. 63).

In the same way, Frankl evaluated his decision to leave the job as a doctor in Bad Woerishofen to look for his mother and wife. This decision was given to him by his conscience: "Because it would be selfish of me to continue working here—even though I would prefer to stay here, where I will be able to work and live in good conditions" (Frankl 2015, p. 45).

The birth of his "spiritual child", the book "The Doctor and the Soul" is considered by him as happiness, which is not complete but highly longed for a long time (Frankl 2015). He wrote the following about his inner state during the time: "This was the only thing that seemed worthwhile to me, and I buried myself in work" (Frankl 2000, p. 105).

The first time Frankl found joy after his return to Vienna was talking on the radio about the suicide: "Last week I talked on the radio, about suicide. Supposedly I have a clear microphone voice. Have received many enthusiastic letters from unknown persons, from whole hospital rooms in the hospital for incurables etc. The first time that I felt joy since my return to Vienna!" (Frankl 2015, pp. 62–63). Feedback and positive results may seem to have encouraged Frankl and given him a sense of meaningfulness.

Frankl also gave his second wife Elly Schwindt the particular role in his psychological recovery: Frankl described her as a person "who was able to turn everything around in one fell swoop" (Frankl 2015, p. 72). After the engagement with Elly, Frankl wrote that he finally had someone who took care of him "in all things" and "with all the love" (Frankl 2015, p. 84).

After the habilitation in the medical Dean of the University of Vienna and first successes of the books "The Doctor and the Soul" and "The Psychologist survives the Concentration Camp" (later "The Man's Search For Meaning") Frankl found the meaning of life again. He saw purpose in his survival, and he was fulfilled with doing his job as lecturer and author of books (Frankl 2015).

The descriptions above show the following motives in Viktor Frankl's life after the release from a concentration camp: living according to own conscience and moral values, fulfilling his tasks and duties (such as publishing books, giving lectures), faith to God. The popularity of the books and meeting with Elly Schwindt contributed to the psychological recovery of Viktor Frankl. Since then, he was able again to see his life purpose and meaning as he could again to actualize himself by sharing his experiences in lectures, books about logotherapy, and working as a doctor.

6.4 Alexander's Indicators of Psychological Salience

Examples of Alexander's indicators of psychological salience (see Sect. 5.4.2) are used to analyze and interpret key aspects of "The Man's Search For Meaning" (Frankl 1984), while the autobiographical work is understood as a direct expression of the individual researched.

Frequency
The most frequent topic Frankl regarded in his book is spiritual development. Frankl reported that he had been impressed by improvised prayers and services in the camp he has never seen before (Frankl 1984). He also reported about a spiritualistic séance, which was illegally organized in a camp (Frankl 1984). Frankl frequently wrote about spiritual freedom which could make the person resilient towards any suffering (Frankl 1984). Frankl frequently addressed the topic of meaning and purpose in life. He saw the meaning and purpose due to enjoyment and creativeness as well as suffering, fate and death (Frankl 1984). So, he began to search for meaning and helped his fellow-prisoners achieve the same. In order to find the meaning, Frankl made himself aware of his present situation which could have been even worse; he directed his thoughts toward the better future where everything can be possible and addressed the meaning of the past experiences (Frankl 1984).

Emphasis
In his book, Frankl described three emotional reactions to the camp life in Auschwitz. The second phase is the state of apathy, which meant for the prisoner emotional death (Frankl 1984). The newly arrived prisoner experienced the most painful emotions, all of which he tried to deaden. Frankl described the phase of apathy mostly detailed compared to other two emotional states, depicting the apathetic state of his co-prisoners (Frankl 1984) and his emotional indifference (Frankl 1984).

Another emphasis is based on the notion of human's freedom of will and attitude in every situation. Frankl believed that spiritual freedom, as well as the independence of the mind, could be preserved under every circumstance (Frankl 1984).

Primacy
Frankl started his book with the preface talking about the immense popularity of his book all over the world. Frankl claimed that this book had had three editions (the year 1984), has been translated into 19 languages and "the English editions have sold almost two and a half million copies" (Frankl 1984, p. 15). Although from the first line Frankl emphasized the great success of his book, he also wrote that the bestseller status of it was not a great achievement for him. He wrote that he regarded the success as a by-product of "personal dedication to a cause greater than oneself" (Frankl 1984, p. 17). However, the researcher suggests that the enormous popularity of his books was still crucial for Frankl, and it helped him to overcome the crisis of the meaning of his life. It seems that Frankl did not like to show or even consciously feel proud of his accomplishments. His emotional side seems to be suppressed by himself. There are no words of gratitude or joy. Instead of it, Frankl stayed rational

and distanced, giving the reader concrete numbers which demonstrated the popularity of the book all over the world.

Isolation

Describing the phase of liberation, Frankl put his attention to camp guards. Before he depicted the experiences and psychological state of the prisoners after and during the liberation, he asked the questions "about the psychological make-up of the camp guards" and "How is it possible that men of flesh and blood could treat others as so many prisoners say they have been treated?" (Frankl 1984, pp. 105). These questions seem not to fit the context of the topic entirely. However, it seems to be essential for Frankl to address this topic as he might have wanted to highlight that "among the guards, there were some sadists, sadists in the purest clinical sense", still there were those who took pity on the prisoners (Frankl 1984, p. 106). Frankl also wrote that some prisoners were even more brutal as some camp guards. Therefore, the position had told nothing about the human qualities of people. According to Frankl human kindness could be found in all groups, even those which would be easy to condemn (Frankl 1984). The researcher suggests that the explanation of the behaviour of prisoners and camp guards was provided in order to convince the reader to regard all members of camp equally looking at their moral and ethical convictions and not at their position in the camp. Probably, Frankl's attitude toward camp guards and prisoners was again shaped by his faith, the idea of good human qualities and forgiveness.

Uniqueness

There were no unique pointers found.

Error, distortion, omission

In the first chapter, Frankl promised to provide the reader with personal experiences from camp life:

> THIS BOOK DOES NOT CLAIM TO BE AN ACCOUNT OF facts and events but of personal experiences, experiences which millions of prisoners have suffered time and again. It is the inside story of a concentration camp, told by one of its survivors (Frankl 1984, p. 21).

Although there are plenty of facts in the book from personal experiences, Franks tended to distance himself and describe the reality using the third-form pronouns or describing the experiences of other prisoners instead of talking in I-Perspective.

The following Table 6.1 illustrates the facts and experiences from the third-person perspective (first column) and aims at finding relevant descriptions from Viktor Frankl's personal experiences (second column):

Incompletion

There were no incompletion pointers found in the book.

Negation

In his recollections about the days of admission and adjustment to the camp reality, Frankl pointed out that he was not shocked by camp conditions and the threat of

6.4 Alexander's Indicators of Psychological Salience

Table 6.1 First- and third-person perspectives

Describing "the facts" from the distance (third-person perspective)	Describing personal experience (first-person perspective)
"Little does he know of the hard fight for existence which raged among the prisoners. This was an unrelenting struggle for daily bread and for life itself, for one's own sake or for that of a good friend" (Frankl 1984, p. 22)	Did Frankl struggle for food? How he experienced it?—No explicit answer
"There was neither time nor desire to consider moral or ethical issues. Every man was controlled by one thought only: to keep himself alive for the family waiting for him at home and to save his friends" (Frankl 1984, p. 23)	Were moral and ethical issues crucial to Frankl at that time?—No explicit answer
"The symptom that characterizes the first phase is shock. Under certain conditions, shock may even precede the prisoner's formal admission to the camp. I shall give as an example the circumstances of my own admission" (Frankl 1984, pp. 26–27)	Was he shocked?—The answer follows later. Frank refers to the words of the friends but does not give his opinion: "Friends whom I have met later have told me that I was not one of those whom the shock of admission greatly depressed" (Frankl 1984, p. 37)
"[…] quite unexpectedly, most of us were overcome by a grim sense of humor. We knew that we had nothing to lose except our so ridiculously naked lives" (Frankl 1984, p. 34)	Did he also have that kind of grim sense of humour?—The answer follows later in the "we"-form: "When the showers started to run, we all tried very hard to make fun, both about ourselves and about each other" (Frankl 1984, pp. 34–35)
	Frankl describes the situation where he was sarcastic demonstrating the braveness: "I even allowed myself to say once to a kindly foreman, 'If you could learn from me how to do a brain operation in as short a time as I am learning this road work from you, I would have great respect for you.' And he grinned" (Frankl 1984, p. 47)
"Apart from that strange kind of humour, another sensation seized us: curiosity" (Frankl 1984, p. 35)	Was he also curious?—Yes, but Frankl did not depict the experiences from camp life. "I have experienced this kind of curiosity before, as a fundamental reaction toward certain strange circumstances. When my life was once endangered by a climbing accident, I felt only one sensation at the critical moment: curiosity, curiosity as to whether I should come out of it alive or with a fractured skull or some other injuries" (Frankl 1984, p. 35)
"Apart from the already described reactions, the newly arrived prisoner experienced the tortures of other most painful emotions, all of which he tried to deaden. First of all, there was his boundless longing for his home and his family. This often could become so acute that he felt	Did he miss the family?—Yes. However, he vividly described his feelings much later (see "vividness"): "That brought thoughts of my own wife to mind" (Frankl 1984, p. 56)

(continued)

Table 6.1 (continued)

Describing "the facts" from the distance (third-person perspective)	Describing personal experience (first-person perspective)
himself consumed by longing" (Frankl 1984, p. 39)	
"Then there was disgust; disgust with all the ugliness which surrounded him, even in its mere external forms. But the prisoner who had passed into the second stage of his psychological reactions did not avert his eyes any more" (Frankl 1984, pp. 39–40)	Did he also lose his feeling of disgust?—Yes. Frankl gives an explicit answer: "After one of them had just died, I watched without any emotional upset the scene that followed, which was repeated over and over again with each death" (Frankl 1984, p. 40)
"Several of my colleagues in the camp who were trained in psychoanalysis often spoke of a "regression" in the camp inmate—a retreat to a more primitive form of mental life. His wishes and desires became obvious in his dreams" (Frankl 1984, pp. 47–48)	Did he also regard himself as primitive?—No specific answer
"The religious interest of the prisoners, as far and as soon as it developed, was the most sincere imaginable. The depth and vigour of religious belief often surprised and moved a new arrival" (Frankl 1984, p. 54)	Did his inner life develop? Did his spiritual life or faith become stronger?—Frankl claimed that he had just a professional interest. However, he recollects his prey to god during his time as a prisoner as well as after liberation: "At that moment there was very little I knew of myself or of the worlds—I had but one sentence in mind—always the same: "I called to the Lord from my narrow prison and He answered me in the freedom of space" (Frankl 1984, p.111) Frankl gives no explicit information about how he regarded his relationships with god as well as his inner spiritual world at that time. Frankl gives no information about his spiritual experiences but still speaks about faith frequently (see frequency)
"We envied those prisoners their relatively well-regulated, secure and happy life" (Frankl 1984, p. 66)	Was he envy?—No explicit answer
"If the man in the concentration camp did not struggle against this in a last effort to save his self-respect, he lost the feeling of being an individual, a being with a mind, with inner freedom and personal value" (Frankl 1984, p. 70)	Did he feel that he lost his self-respect?—no explicit answer
"This state of inner suspense was followed by total relaxation. But it would be quite wrong to think that we went mad with joy" (Frankl 1984, p. 109)	What feelings did he have after liberation if not joy?—No explicit answer
"We had literally lost the ability to feel pleased and had to relearn it slowly" (Frankl 1984, p. 110)	

(continued)

6.5 Schultz's Prototypical Scenes

Table 6.1 (continued)

Describing "the facts" from the distance (third-person perspective)	Describing personal experience (first-person perspective)
"The body has fewer inhibitions than the mind. It made good use of the new freedom from the first moment on. It began to eat ravenously, for hours and days, even half the night" (Frankl 1984, p. 110)	Did he also eat a lot after liberation?—No explicit answer
"It would be an error to think that a liberated prisoner was not in need of spiritual care any more. We have to consider that a man who has been under such enormous mental pressure for such a long time is naturally" (Frankl 1984, p. 111)	How did he fulfil his spiritual hunger after liberation? After liberation, Frankl recalls his prayers to god and connected his personal recovery through the relationship with god: "How long I knelt there and repeated this sentence memory can no longer recall. But I know that on that day, in that hour, my new life started. Step for step, I progressed, until I again became a human being" (Frankl 1984, p. 111)
"Apart from the moral deformity resulting from the sudden release of mental pressure, there were two other fundamental experiences which threatened to damage the character of the liberated prisoner: bitterness and disillusionment when he returned to his former life" (Frankl 1984, p. 112) "When, on his return, a man found that in many places he was met only with a shrug of the shoulders and with hackneyed phrases, he tended to become bitter and to ask himself why he had gone through all that he had" (Frankl 1984, p. 113)	Did he also suffer under bitterness and disillusionment when he returned to his former life?—No specific answer about his feelings

death (Frankl 1984). The researcher suggests that Frankl did not wish to show the reader and himself his "weak" feelings which would not suit the meaning therapy.

The examples of Alexander's indicators of psychological salience provided more in-depth insight into the experience of Viktor Frankl's life during and after the stay in the concentration camps. In the following section, Schultz's prototypical scenes analysis is used to identify pointers, outlined similarly to the ones outlined by Alexander.

6.5 Schultz's Prototypical Scenes

The prototypical scenes identified in Frankl's book "Man's Search For Meaning" are used for the interpretation of his book in order to get a more in-depth insight into the personality of Frankl.

Vividness, specificity, emotional intensity

There are the following topics which Frankl described vividly and emotionally intense:

- Suffering in the camp. However, as mentioned before, Frankl did not depict his "own" suffering but described the suffering of all co-prisoners.
- Recollections of home. Compared to other recollections, Frankl depicted his longing to home in a more personal way using "I"-perspective and showing his emotions and feelings (Frankl 1984).
- Nature beauty. Despite all the sufferings, Frankl felt amazed by nature even at times of suffering (Frankl 1984).
- Dreams about freedom (Frankl 1984).
- Escape and liberation (Frankl 1984).
- Dreams about his wife. Frankl vividly showed his affection and love to his first wife Tilly, who was in another camp. She was one of his purposes to stay alive and overcome all the suffering of the camp life (Frankl 1984).

Interpenetration

Although Frankl did not provide any explicit information about his religious beliefs in the book, the sense of spirituality, higher power, or fate interpenetrates throughout the book. Frankl was sure about the existence of God, who would not have expected to be disappointed (Frankl 1984). Frankl also wrote that he tried to bring other prisoners to an understanding about the existence of somebody "above" whether it is a friend or a wife, or God who expect from them a certain behaviour and decisions (Frankl 1984). Frankl (1984) reported that he had refused to cross his name off the death list in the concentration camp in order "to let fate take its course" (Frankl 1984, p. 75). After being released, he often quoted the Holy Scripture in order to keep his will to stay alive and not to give up (Frankl 1984); he offered the support to other survivals persuading him that they would see their relatives in Heaven (Frankl 1984).

Thrownness

Frankl described the violated status quo in terms of losing the meaning of life after the liberation and deep frustration facing a new reality. Frankl wrote that the former prisoners had no feelings for joy when they were released (Frankl 1984) as they lost their ability to feel pleased and had to relearn it (Frankl 1984).

The other fundamental experience of thrownness was the feeling of bitterness when the prisoner returned to his former life. Frankl pointed out the mental pressure of not been understood by others when he talked about all the sufferings the prisoners went through (Frankl 1984).

Another experience was disillusionment, the destruction of hope that after the liberation from the camp, the life would be better (Frankl 1984) Frankl emphasized that the newly released prisoner experienced high mental pressure and his spiritual hunger became stronger (Frankl 1984).

Again, Frankl did not describe his experience personally from personal I-Perspective. He often distanced himself describing other released prisoners or using "we-form". Frankl omitted telling how he personally nourished his spiritual hunger after release, the only detail he gave was a spontaneous praying in the meadows (Frankl 1984).

6.6 Chapter Conclusion

The life course of Viktor Frankl has been analyzed in chronological order from his childhood, adolescent years, including the life in concentration camps and his life after the release. The researcher concentrated on identifying the transcendent virtues which shaped the Frankl's personality, worldview and decisions as well as the structure of meaning according to the PURE-Model of Paul Wong (2012) throughout different stages of Frankl's life. Alexander's indicators of psychological saliency as well as Schultz's prototypical scenes were used to interpret key aspects of "The Man's Search For Meaning" as well as to get a deeper insight into a personality of Viktor Frankl.

References

Frankl, V.E. 1984. *Man's search for meaning*. New York, NY: Pocket Books.
———. 2000. *Viktor Frankl. Recollections. An autobiography*. Cambridge: Basic Books.
———. 2015. *Es kommt der Tag, da bist du frei*. München: Kösel-Verlag.
Längle, A. 2013. *Viktor Frankl: Eine Begegnung*. Wien: facultas.wuv.
Pattakos, A.N. 2010. *Prisoners of our thoughts. Viktor Frankl's principles for discovering meaning in life and work*. 2nd ed. San Francisco: Berrett-Koehler.
Peterson, C., and M.E.P. Seligman. 2004. *Character strengths and virtues*. Washington, DC: American Psychological Association: Hoffman.
Wong, P.T.P. 2012. Toward a dual-system model of what makes life Worth living. In *The human quest for meaning. Theories, research and applications*, ed. P.T.P. Wong, 3–22. New York, NY: Routledge.

Chapter 7
Discussion of Results

7.1 Chapter Preview

In this chapter, the results of Viktor Frankl's life are described according to two tenets of PP 2.0 of Paul Wong (2011, 2019, 2020a, b). These are virtue and meaning. Each tenet will be discussed in detail to facilitate an understanding of Viktor Frankl's life and to ascertain the effectiveness of Wong's theory in enhancing the positive and managing the negative life experiences in order to increase well-being and decrease mental illnesses.

7.2 The Virtue of Transcendence

This section provides information on how the character strengths of transcendent virtues might have enhanced optimal human functioning in Viktor Frankl's life. Moreover, it shows how transcendent character strengths might have provided Viktor Frankl with a sense of meaning in life despite suffering and crises. In the following, the virtue of transcendence is divided into its character strengths and discussed in detail during Viktor Frankl's life.

7.2.1 Appreciation of Beauty

It was fundamental for Viktor Frankl to recognize, acknowledge and value positive character strengths of the people who surrounded him and feel a positive connection about it. He highly appreciated the character traits of his father and mother. Despite potential severity, his father represented for Frankl an excellent example of a just and loving person whom he always wanted to emulate. The researcher suggests that

Frankl's feeling of respect and positive connection toward his father, who was stoic and religious in behaviour, might have promoted his resiliency and deep spirituality. His mother embodied for him emotional warmth and goodness and might have contributed to the development of his emotional intelligence. His first wife Tilly also impressed Viktor Frankl not just by her appearance, but her character, especially intuition and kindness. The awareness of positive traits of Frankl's family members might have enabled him to stay connected to them.

Frankl was also aware of the beauty of art and nature. Being in the concentration camp, he enjoyed the music in the evening and contemplated the beauty of nature mindfully. The hostile reality of that time did not discourage him from finding the positives, which might contribute to his emotional well-being being and the relief of his stress.

7.2.2 Gratitude

Viktor Frankl tended to omit expressing his stance of gratitude explicitly. In only one letter, he mentioned that he was grateful for being able to work according to his abilities and inclinations. Frankl tended to describe fortunate life events emotionlessly describing the positive traits of person or situation (see "appreciation of beauty"). The researcher suggests that the reason for it might have laid in the character traits of Frankl who tended to distance himself from his strong emotions describing life events cognitively. Moreover, Viktor Frankl might not have desired to portray plenty of happy moments in his life as he aimed to stay independent from fortune in life and persuade his readers to do the same.

The stance of thankfulness is noticeable in Viktor Frankl's life during his stay in a concentration camp and after his release. He was thankful for the opportunity to experience the suffering and have survived. The researcher suggests that such a stance enabled Viktor Frankl to accept his reality and find out its usefulness for him, which might contribute to his readiness to overcome challenges.

7.2.3 Hope

Frankl seems to have had a strong cognitive and motivational stance toward the future resulting in his expecting the best and working to achieve it. The hope for a better result encouraged Viktor Frankl to sometimes undertake even risky steps to complete the result. Therefore, Viktor Frankl's hope made him proactive.

Being in a concentration camp, Frankl seemed to practice hope consciously. He distanced himself from camp circumstances and suffering and imagined a better future as a lecturer at university and with his first wife, Tilly. The hope that she would stay alive guided Viktor Frankl through desperate circumstances.

7.2 The Virtue of Transcendence

After he found out that his mother and the wife had not survived, he lost his sense of life and hope for a good life. During this period, no more positive remarks regarding hope for a better future were to be found in his letters and books. However, the researcher suggests that the loss of two people close to him enabled Viktor Frankl to arrive at a more profound sense of hope. Whereas his initial hope was connected to the particular outcome (the good life with Tilly), the hope in the period after liberation from the concentration camp seems to be transcendent. Frankl believed that his former and present suffering had had meaning, and they served a particular goal which he could not comprehend at those times. His hope became the source of a daily commitment towards his duties as an author and a doctor.

After Frankl's books became popular and after meeting with his second wife Elly, the narrative of positive hope and faith occurred in Frankl's letters again which implies that Frankl was still influenced by positive feedback and own success. However, he tried to hide it publicly (see "negation").

7.2.4 Humour

It was typical for Viktor Frankl to see the world through humour and wit. As a university lecturer, he playfully created incongruities making others smile and laugh and keeping the interest of his audience. In his private life, he was also a humorous person. During the life in Auschwitz, Frankl as other prisoners used to compose ironical or even sarcastic views on adversity that allowed them to diminish their fear of possible death and release their bitter feelings.

There were no bon mots after Frankl got to know about Tilly's and mother's death. After getting to know Elly Schwindt and after the success of his book "The Doctor and the Soul", Frankl started writing ironical and humorous letters again. Therefore, Frankl used jokes in order to alter his perception of danger and release distressful feelings.

7.2.5 Spirituality

Since childhood, Frankl asked himself about the purpose of life and death, finding for himself satisfactory answers which shaped his decisions and behaviour. He had a coherent belief about the higher purpose and meaning of life. He was convinced that every person should ask themselves to find an answer to the question of what makes their life meaningful. Frankl was convinced that suffering and even death still served the higher purpose; therefore, all life events are meaningful within the larger scheme of things.

These beliefs might have influenced his interpretations of life events and resulted in persistence in overcoming difficulties and life challenges. His religiousness and faith in God seem to significantly contribute to his views of positive and negative life events as well as his decision-making. Frankl aimed to live according to his conscience, fulfilling the biblical commandments and facing danger and even death with the belief that he was under the protection of a higher power. The researcher noticed that Frankl cultivated in himself such traits and attitudes as humbleness, acceptance of his own fate as God's will. It resulted in trust toward the future, doing good deeds not for his own sake but for the prosperity of others, readiness to sacrifice the most important things, spiritual freedom from any given circumstances, transcendent love as the highest purpose. These ideas, which seem to have a biblical origin, also become the core points of logotherapy.

The researcher also concluded that spirituality and faith enabled Viktor Frankl to re-understand his life-meaning after the loss of his mother and first wife. He seems to have stayed faithful to God, believing that his life could contribute to the prosperity of others. The decision to write and publish his books gave him the feeling of duty, which made him resilient toward misfortune and negative experiences. The stance of humility and trust in God enabled Frankl not to be worried about the future, as he believed that God would arrange everything.

7.3 Meaning

This section provides the in-depth insight on the process of meaning-making in the life of Viktor Frankl according to the PURE-Modell of Paul Wong (see Sect. 4.3.3), as well as how character strengths of transcendent virtue (see above) and the process of meaning-making are interconnected.

7.3.1 Purpose

Viktor Frankl believed in a person's responsibility for their existence and necessity to answer the question of the meaning of life on their own. Already as a teenager, Frankl understood that his life purpose was transcendent and served a higher goal which he probably could not comprehend. His faith and spirituality might have strengthened this point of view and enabled him not to rationally explain all life events but have trust in the higher power he believed, which enhanced his well-being and resiliency.

In his adolescent years, Frankl developed three possible courses of action for finding life meaning: through deeds, the experience of values through one medium (beauty through arts, etc.) and a change of attitude. These three ways seem to be transcendent. According to Frankl, deeds should serve the well-being of others; the experience makes the person forget themselves and connect to the experienced object; change of attitude makes the person free from any given (unfavourable) circumstances. These ideas seem to have lived through and deepened throughout all life stages of Frankl's life. The researcher concludes that such character strengths as spirituality and appreciation of beauty helped him to define his existential values, overall direction and life goals which shaped his daily decisions and helped him to overcome negative experiences in the concentration camp.

7.3.2 Understanding

It is striking that already as a child, Frankl thought about suffering and its meaning, although there were no examples of his suffering found in this life's period. The research proposes that Frankl's possible fear or frustration about death might have brought him strong negative emotions which he tried to resolve. In order to find a satisfactory answer on the questions of transitory nature of life and possibly to manage his negative feelings, he might have pursued the self-understanding and self-knowledge in the larger scheme of things which promoted the meaning-making process.

After finding answers for himself about the general meaning of life and death (see purpose), Frankl was able to find satisfactory answers and interpretations on specific life events, positive experiences and suffering. Such an attitude enhanced Frankl's motivation to stay resilient and aim to overcome the challenges of camp life and those after his release.

The researcher also suggests that Frankl's ability to recognize the meaning of negative emotions (shame about surviving or deep frustration concerning Tilly's death) enabled Frankl to accept the negatives and use them as a tool for positive changes which will be described in the next section.

7.3.3 Responsible Action

Frankl's values, understanding of the situations and their consequences on other people resulted in responsible actions. Reading the books and personal letters of Viktor Frankl, the researcher concluded that his life choices and actions, especially in challenging situations, were shaped by his spirituality (including faith), hope, appreciation of beauty, gratitude and humour. These character strengths enabled him to face negative experiences and regard them as something meaningful, which is worthy of experiencing and overcoming.

Frankl's spirituality and religiousness enabled him to undertake risky steps which even allowed him to confront death (the decision to stay in Vienna with his parents, the decision not to flee from a camp when an opportunity was offered). Frankl seems to have behaved according to his sense of conscience and fairness, and not by his own interests. Moreover, these character strengths enabled Frankl to see the meaning of negatives, develop acceptance toward unchangeable situations and the sense of duty toward his life tasks, in particular when the hope for a better future was undeniably lost.

Frankl's sense of humour enabled him to diminish his fears, especially in the concentration camp, and resulted in a calmer stance toward any difficulties he experienced and curiosity he felt about the future.

7.3.4 Enjoyment and Evaluation

Viktor Frankl seems to have felt positive feelings from doing the things which were good and corresponded to his ethical principles and religious beliefs. Even if the decision or action failed (such as loss of a manuscript for a book in a concentration camp, death of his family members), he felt satisfied that he could do everything accordingly to his capacities. After the loss of hope for a better future, Frankl reevaluated his life purpose (fulfilling his "duties" as an author). Therefore, failures were regarded by Viktor Frankl as opportunities for positive changes which made him flexible and strengthened his beliefs. He stayed faithful regarding his core values, changing his course of actions according to the situation.

7.4 Alexander's Indicators of Psychological Salience

Examples of Alexander's indicators of psychological salience were used in this psychobiography to analyze and interpret key aspects of "The Man's Search For Meaning" (Frankl 1984). In this section, the results will be discussed and commented.

Frequency

In his book "Man's Search For Meaning", Frankl repeatedly turned to the topic of spiritual development and faith. Viktor Frankl seems to have been a deeply religious person whose life actions decisions, as well as logotherapeutic ideas, were shaped by his faith. It might have given him a sense of security and knowledge that his actions were "right".

By reading the book "Man's Search For Meaning", the researcher noticed that all actions as well feelings were interpreted through the question of meaningfulness and purpose. The researcher proposes that Frankl, as a highly reflective person, might have been able to notice hidden connections between life events and how those life events, even negative ones, positively influenced his life in the future. It might strengthen his belief that everything in life has its purpose, which might have made him resilient towards suffering.

Emphasis

In his book, Frankl meticulously described the state of apathy during the stay in a concentration camp, which he and other prisoners experienced. The researcher believes that this time was the most challenging for Viktor Frankl as his ability to recognize life meaning was under pressure. However, Frankl was able to overcome this phase by believing in inner freedom of will and attitude in every situation. This human ability was also emphasized by Frankl as a tool to overcome every difficult situation in life.

Primacy

Although Viktor Frankl described himself as a person who did not aim at achieving success, in the preface of his book, he meticulously described its immense popularity all over the world. The researcher suggests that the feelings of intense happiness or pride might have been unacceptable for Viktor Frankl; therefore, he tried to suppress or hide them. According to his ideas, he believed that outer circumstances should not influence a person and serve as a reason for their life choices. His idea of spiritual freedom seems to be manifested in emotional distance and neutrality, even towards positive life events. Frankl often used to describe his accomplishments talking about facts and numbers and avoiding any descriptions of his emotional state. Therefore, the researcher suggests that Frankl was still an ambitious person trying to achieve the best result and feedback while staying emotionally distant.

Isolation

It seems to be essential for Viktor Frankl to forgive those who brought him suffering. Therefore, he suddenly tackled the question of the brutality of the camp guard before describing the phase of liberation from concentration camps. Probably, Frankl raised this question within the phase of liberation as he unconsciously aimed at gaining psychological freedom from camp guards by understanding them.

Error, Distortion, Omission

In his book, Frankl often refrained from describing his own experiences and feelings. He used to describe experiences of other prisoners and to convey his feelings as well as thoughts through shared experience. Moreover, he did not say anything explicitly about his faith, his feelings about God and his relationship to him. Instead of this, Frankl tended to depict his transcendent experiences through the actions, avoiding descriptions of his emotions. These facts show again that Frankl tended to avoid topics of his feelings, vulnerabilities and fears and aimed at staying objective. Such an attitude enabled him not to be overthrown by the intense emotions of frustration, fear or disappointment.

Negation

As mentioned before, Viktor Frankl avoided speaking about his "weak" feelings. He stated that he had not been shocked by the camp reality. It seems to be important for Viktor Frankl not to admit his "human weakness" before larger groups of people and keep inner spiritual freedom despite every circumstance. The researcher suggests that Frankl's ability to stay emotionally neutral had two sides. On the one hand, it might have made him more resilient toward suffering as he was able to distance himself from the circumstances. On the other hand, he might have been unable to feel and express strong positive emotions, such as happiness, pleasure and gratitude.

7.5 Schultz's Prototypical Scenes

Vividness, Specificity, Emotional Intensity
The topics which Viktor Frankl described as emotionally intense might have to say what he believed and appreciated the most during the stay in the concentration camp. He vividly and meticulously described the life and suffering of prisoners. This fact might implicate such traits of Frankl as empathy, tendency to reflect on outer life events and conditions avoiding concentrating much on own negative feelings. Frankl described vividly and emotionally intensely his memories of home, his wife, as well as his dreams about freedom. These thoughts might have served him as a hope for a better future and as a motivation to survive.

Interpenetration
Frankl's memories of his life in the book "Man's Search For Meaning" are interpenetrated by his own religious belief which he, however, never confessed explicitly. The researcher suggests that his interpretation of life events is strongly shaped by his religiosity and such attitudes as acceptance of God's will, obedience and importance of good deeds for others. His fear of death was weakened as he might have believed in the eternal existence of the soul. The suffering seems to be regarded by Frankl as a trial which leads to spiritual freedom from any outer conditions and a stronger connection to God. Practising trust and acceptance, Frankl was able to believe in a purpose in every adverse condition.

Thrownness
The new reality after liberation challenged Frankl's ability to see the hidden purpose of every problematic circumstance. His hopes for a better future were destroyed. It required from him re-understanding of his life-purpose and taking a new course of actions. Frankl seemed to return to his former strategies of interpretation of life from religious as well as logotherapeutic perspective practising humility, trust and acceptance.

7.6 Conclusion

This chapter discussed Viktor Frankl's life structure, according to Wong's theory of PP2.0 (2011). According to this theory, the positive and negative life events should be integrated in order to enhance the resiliency and well-being of a person. Two tenets of this theory, such as virtue and meaning, provided the guideline in describing Viktor Frankl's life. It was meticulously described how transcendent character strengths such as appreciation of beauty, gratitude, hope, humour and spirituality contributed to Frank's ability to identify the meaning of negative life events and stay resilient towards suffering. The structure of meaning in Viktor Frankl's life was additionally discussed according to the PURE-Model of Wong (2012). The following chapter will bring the study to a conclusion, and further recommendations for research will be provided.

References

Frankl, V.E. 1984. *Man's search for meaning*. New York, NY: Pocket Books.

Wong, P.T.P. 2011. Positive psychology 2.0: Towards a balanced interactive model of the good life. *Canadian Psychology/Psychologie Canadienne* 52: 69–81. https://doi.org/10.1037/a0022511.

———. 2012. Toward a dual-system model of what makes life Worth living. In *The human quest for meaning. Theories, research and applications*, ed. P.T.P. Wong, 3–22. New York, NY: Routledge.

———. 2019. Second wave positive psychology's (PP 2.0) contribution to counselling psychology, [special issue]. *Counselling Psychology Quarterly*. https://doi.org/10.1080/09515070.2019.1671320.

———. 2020a. The maturing of positive psychology and the emerging PP 2.0: A book review of positive psychology (3rd ed.) by William Compton and Edward Hoffman. *International Journal of Wellbeing* 10 (1): 107–117. https://doi.org/10.5502/ijw.v10i1.885.

———. 2020b. *Made for resilience and happiness: Effective coping with COVID-19 according to Viktor E. Frankl and Paul T. P. Wong*. Toronto: INPM Press.

Chapter 8
Conclusions

8.1 Chapter Preview

This final chapter includes a summary of the research and addresses the limitations of this psychobiographical research on Viktor Frankl. After that, the value of this research is discussed, and the recommendations for further research are provided. This study is then drawn to an end with the conclusions of the findings proposed.

8.2 Summary of the Research Findings

PP2.0 integrates both positive and negative experiences as well as the strengths and weaknesses of people. This approach enables the person to understand the complexity of life in its totality as well as accepting their responsibility for life and dealing with negative experiences and suffering as they are the necessary part of life and humanity's development. In this research, the first two tenets of PP 2.0, such as virtue and meaning, were followed throughout Viktor Frank's life, during his childhood and adolescent years, especially before, during and after his stay in concentration camps. Since childhood, Viktor Frankl developed a deep sense of life-meaning despite every negative circumstance, and he believed that negative life experiences are worth living through, as they served a higher purpose and goal.

Wong's assertion that suffering and enhancement of happiness should be regarded as interdependent endeavours has been strongly supported in this study. Frankl's life decisions demonstrate that suffering can be a source of fulfilment if individuals recognise their responsibility and spiritual freedom from any given circumstances, as well as the higher purpose of every life event.

Two tenets of PP2.0, such as virtue and meaning, are demonstrated in this study on the life of Viktor Frankl. The virtue of transcendence was chosen to highlight the necessity to cultivate it in a person, with special regard to character strengths, as an appreciation of beauty, gratitude, hope, humour, spirituality as they help to recognize the meaning of every difficult situation and stay resilient in suffering. The PURE-Model of Wong (2012) was used to describe the structure of meaning and to indicate how transcendent character strengths shaped Frankl's interpretations of life allowing him to recognize the meaning of suffering and act according to his world understanding and values.

This study also demonstrates an in-depth analysis of Viktor Frankl's personality according to Alexander's indicators of psychological saliency and Schultz's prototypical scenes. It illuminates his character traits which were not recognised by him personally, as well as possible side effects of his character strengths, abilities and decisions.

8.3 The Limitations of this Research

The methodological considerations relevant to psychobiographical research were presented and discussed in Chap. 5 of this study. This study on Viktor Frankl, however, has to acknowledge its constraints. As there was limited scope to research the life of Viktor Frankl, little attention could be given to the scientific works that he produced, as well as his life in old age. This information would have been able to provide additional insight into the personality of Viktor Frankl, as well as possible interactions between PP2.0 and logotherapy.

Additionally, there was little information analysed from Frankl's relatives and colleagues. Thus, the information could not be confirmed, compared or disputed. As the theory chosen for this research is a PP2.0, the focus of the information obtained in this study pertained to Viktor Frankl's ability to overcome negative life events, as well as integrate both positive and negative life experiences. This study has, therefore, only focused on selected and clearly pre-defined aspects of his life, and can in no way account for his whole, entire and holistic life experience.

8.4 The Value of this Research

This research has evaluated the theoretical content of PP2.0 of Paul Wong (2011). It has studied the life of Viktor Frankl. It has served to illustrate Wong's proposal to discover benefits or potentials of negative outcomes in order to overcome suffering and increase well-being (Wong 2020a, b).

Additionally, necessary elements of meaning were analysed and gave a detailed explanation of Viktor Frankl's core values, life understanding, his actions and its evaluation. This study also highlighted the link between transcendent virtue and resiliency as the character strengths of transcendent virtues helped Viktor Frankl recognise the meaning of difficult situations and believe in the ultimate purpose of his life. It also offered an in-depth analysis of the personality of Viktor Frankl and disputed his unconscious character traits and aspirations.

8.5 Recommendations for Further Research

This study demonstrated that the virtue of transcendence and the meaning-making process are crucial components in overcoming life difficulties and challenges. Therefore, this study might be motivating further future research of these character strengths to enhance a person's ability to overcome suffering.

Moreover, other tenets of PP2.0, such as resiliency and well-being, could provide further information on the life of Viktor Frankl and his ability to enjoy the positive sides of life and overcome the negative ones.

A more in-depth study of Frankl's childhood, as well as his other scientific works, could be an object of further research to obtain additional clarity and information concerning his personal development and life decisions. It would add to the validity of the research findings in this study.

8.6 Conclusion

This psychobiography illustrated the theory of PP2.0 (Wong 2011) on the example of Viktor Frankl's life. The link between resiliency, virtue and meaning was analysed and interpreted, contributing to the development of the theoretical constructs of this psychological theory. This chapter provided a summary of the study and addressed the limitations and value of this psychobiographical research. The recommendations for further research were provided.

References

Wong, P.T.P. 2011. Positive psychology 2.0: Towards a balanced interactive model of the good life. *Canadian Psychology/Psychologie Canadienne* 52: 69–81. https://doi.org/10.1037/a0022511.
———. 2012. Toward a dual-system model of what makes life Worth living. In *The human quest for meaning. Theories, research and applications*, ed. P.T.P. Wong, 3–22. New York, NY: Routledge.
———. 2020a. The maturing of positive psychology and the emerging PP 2.0: A book review of positive psychology (3rd ed.) by William Compton and Edward Hoffman. *International Journal of Wellbeing* 10 (1): 107–117. https://doi.org/10.5502/ijw.v10i1.885.
———. 2020b. *Made for resilience and happiness: Effective coping with COVID-19 according to Viktor E. Frankl and Paul T. P. Wong*. Toronto: INPM Press.

CPSIA information can be obtained
at www.ICGtesting.com
Printed in the USA
LVHW081312040521
686351LV00025B/537